Acknowledgements

We would like to thank everybody who contributed to the surveys and the production of this report. We were supported by our specialist colleagues in OPCS who carried out the sampling, fieldwork, coding and the complex computing operations. We are grateful for the support and guidance of our colleagues in the Department of Health and Social Security for whom the surveys were carried out.

We are particularly grateful for the co-operation of many people, for example, in universities and hospitals and voluntary organisations who helped in the design of the research project and acted as judges in the disability scaling exercises.

Finally, we would like to thank all the people with disabilities and their carers for their participation in our survey.

Jean Martin
Howard Meltzer
David Elliot

Social Survey Division
OPCS

September 1988

Notes on the tables

Percentages have been rounded to the nearest whole number and as a result may add to between 99 and 101. The total is still shown as 100. Percentages of less than one per cent are shown as 0; cells with no cases are indicated by −.

Base numbers are given in italics. Where a base number is less than 30 statistics have not been given.

OFFICE OF POPULATION CENSUSES AND SURVEYS
SOCIAL SURVEY DIVISION

OPCS surveys of disability in Great Britain
Report 1

The prevalence of disability among adults

Jean Martin
Howard Meltzer
David Elliot

London: Her Majesty's Stationery Office

© *Crown copyright 1988*
First published 1988
Second impression 1989

ISBN 0 11 691229 4

Contents

List of the tables

List of the figures

Summary

The OPCS surveys of disability in Great Britain were commissioned by the DHSS in 1984. They aim to provide up-to-date information about the number of disabled people in Great Britain with different levels of severity and their circumstances for the purposes of planning benefits and services. Four separate surveys were carried out between 1985 and 1988, covering adults in private households, children in private households, adults in communal establishments and children in communal establishments.

The results of the surveys are being presented in a series of reports of which this is the first. It describes the main concepts and methods common to all the surveys and presents the prevalence estimates from the two surveys of disabled adults.

Chapter 2 summarises the concepts and methods used to identify people with disabilities for the surveys, the development of a measure of severity of disability and the procedures for obtaining national prevalence estimates. The second part of the report, Chapters 5 to 8, describes each of these in greater detail. Chapter 3 presents the prevalence estimates and Chapter 4 gives information about the characteristics of the disabled adults living in private households and in communal establishments.

The survey focuses on disability, a restriction or lack of ability to perform normal activities, which has resulted from the impairment of a structure or function of the body or mind. As far as possible the surveys attempted to cover all types of disability, whatever their origin. Disability is taken as a continuum in terms of severity, ranging from very slight to very severe. The prevalence estimates therefore depend on the level of severity above which people are counted as disabled for the purposes of the surveys. It was decided to use a relatively low threshold of disability in order to obtain information about people over a wide range of severity. This decision necessarily leads to high prevalence estimates in total, so it is important to examine also how they vary by level of severity.

The survey distinguished thirteen different types of disability (based on those distinguished in the International Classification of Impairments Disabilities and Handicaps) and gives estimates of the numbers of adults with each type. The majority of adults, particularly the more severely disabled and almost all of those living in communal establishments, had more than one type of disability. The most common type was locomotion disabilities, followed by hearing and personal care disabilities.

Information was collected from survey respondents about the nature of the complaints giving rise to their disabilities. While this information was often rather vague, as far as possible complaints were assigned to categories based on the International Classification of Diseases. The survey showed that, among disabled adults living in private households, musculo-skeletal complaints, notably arthritis, were the most commonly cited cause of disability. Ear complaints, eye complaints and diseases of the circulatory system were also commonly mentioned. For those living in communal establishments mental complaints, particularly senile dementia, were mentioned most often, followed by complaints of the musculo-skeletal (arthritis) and nervous systems (strokes).

An innovatory feature of the surveys was the construction of an overall measure of severity of disability which can be used to classify people with different numbers and types of disabilities. In essence, the severity of disability in the thirteen different areas of disability is first established and then the three highest of the thirteen separate scores are combined to give an overall score from which people are allocated to one of ten overall severity categories (category 1 least severe, category 10 most severe).

The survey estimates that there are just over 6 million adults with one or more disabilities in Great Britain, of whom around 400 thousand (or 7%) live in some kind of communal establishment. Almost 14% of adults living in private households have at least one disability. This is a substantially higher estimate than that obtained by the last national survey of the disabled which took place in 1969, but does not necessarily indicate an increase in disability or an under-estimate by the previous survey. The current survey has included people whose disabilities stem from mental illness and handicap who were explicitly not covered by the previous survey and has also included people at a lower level of severity, both of which will contribute to higher estimates. The current survey estimates are, however, lower than those obtained from the General Household Survey of people with a long-standing health problem or disability that affects their activities (21% of adults in private households). However, the latter survey does not specify which activities are to be considered nor how severely they are limited and so its results are not as precise.

The survey shows that over one million adults were assigned to the lowest severity category (1), almost all of whom were living in private households. Successively smaller numbers were found in each higher category. Thus 200 thousand were in the highest category (10), of whom half lived in private households and half in communal establishments.

Many disabilities are caused by the impairments that arise as a consequence of the aging process. It is therefore not surprising that the survey found that the overall rate of disability rises with age, slowly at first then accelerating after 50 and rising very steeply after about 70. Almost 70% of disabled adults were aged 60 or over and indeed nearly half were aged 70 or over. Among those living in communal establishments the proportion of elderly disabled residents was very high: half were aged 80 or over.

Among the most severely disabled adults, (those in severity categories 9 and 10), the very elderly predominate. The rate of disability at this level of severity did not rise steeply until age 70, and rose very steeply after 80. Altogether 64% of adults with this degree of severity were aged 70 or over; 41% were aged 80 or over. Among those living in communal establishments 55% of those in the highest two severity categories were aged 80 or over.

The survey showed that there are more disabled women than men, partly because women live longer than men and therefore there are greater numbers of elderly women among whom disability rates are high. But among those aged 75 or over, the rate of disability, which allows for differing numbers of men and women in the population, is higher for women than for men, indicating that elderly women are more likely to be disabled than elderly men.

Comparisons of disability rates for different regions, standardised for differences in their age distributions, showed that the North, Wales and Yorkshire and Humberside had the highest rates while the southern regions (the GLC area, the South East, East Anglia and the South West) had lower than average rates.

Part I The prevalence of disability among adults

1 Background, aims and coverage of the surveys

1.1 Background

The last national survey of disability in Great Britain took place in 1969. Since then many changes had occurred and the information from that survey, which in any case was limited in scope, could no longer give an accurate description of the current situation. By 1983 there was no up-to-date information giving an overall picture of people in Great Britain with disabilities and their circumstances, and information was required to help form policies for benefits and services for disabled people. Thus in 1983 discussions began between DHSS and OPCS about a programme of survey research to provide the information required.

The 1969 survey was of adults with physical handicaps and impairments living in private households. From the outset DHSS required the new research to differ from the 1969 survey in several respects:

(i) Children, as well as adults were to be covered.

(ii) People living in various forms of communal establishments as well as in private households were to be included.

(iii) The surveys would cover people with all types of disabilities.

(iv) The key concept for the research would be disability, rather than impairment or handicap (see Chapter 2 for definitions).

The changes in the scope of the new study compared with the 1969 survey meant that a considerably higher proportion of the population would be included as disabled than had been included as handicapped or impaired under the definitions used previously.

Following preliminary discussions, development and feasibility work took place in 1984. Ultimately DHSS commissioned OPCS to carry out four separate surveys of:

(a) disabled adults living in private households

(b) disabled children living in private households

(c) disabled adults living in communal establishments

(d) disabled children living in communal establishments

The surveys of disabled adults and children living in private households took place in 1985, following a preliminary screening stage to identify samples for these surveys. The survey of adults in communal establishments took place in 1986 and that of disabled children in communal establishments in 1988.

1.2 Aims of the surveys

The main aims of the surveys of disabled adults and children living in private households were to provide:

(i) comprehensive estimates of the prevalence of disability by age, degree of severity and type of disability;

(ii) information about the financial and social consequences of disability, in particular sources and levels of income and the nature and levels of extra costs arising because of disability; also the effect of disability on employment and mobility;

(iii) some information about the use of and need for health and personal social services.

The survey of disabled children aimed in addition:

(iv) to monitor the implementation of the 1981 Education Act;

(v) to assess the effect of the child's disability on the family, and the responsiveness of services;

(vi) to find out whether there are discontinuities in service provision during adolescence;

(vii) to obtain parents' views of how the services deal with the early indications that their children have health problems.

Although only 2% of all adults live in some kind of communal establishment, many of them are there because they are disabled. Consequentially substantial proportions of disabled adults live in such establishments. The main aim of the surveys of disabled adults and children living in communal establishments was to supplement estimates of the extent and severity of disability provided by the household surveys, enabling overall estimates of disability for the whole population to be calculated by combining the results of the different surveys, suitably weighted.

Subsidiary aims for the surveys of people living in communal establishments included providing information about the use of aids and appliances, health and social services and about the management of financial affairs.

1.3 Follow-up surveys and associated research

Apart from the main surveys other issues have been studied by following up and re-interviewing some of

Fig 1.1 Timetable for the research

Year	Private households		Communal establishments	
	Adults	Children	Adults	Children
1983	discussion background research			
1984	feasibility pilot	discussion		
1985	screening interviewing	screening pilot interviewing	discussion	
1986	coding editing scaling	coding editing	pilot interviewing	discussion
1987	scaling analysis writing	scaling	coding editing analysis writing	pilot
1988	analysis reporting	analysis reporting	analysis reporting	interviewing coding editing analysis reporting

those already interviewed. Three studies have been undertaken by other organisations and are being reported separately:

(i) Twelve- to twenty-year-olds were re-interviewed to examine their transition to adulthood (Social Policy Research Unit, University of York).

(ii) A small number of the people caring for disabled people were interviewed in depth to complement information obtained about them on the main survey (Social Policy Research Unit, University of York).

(iii) The severely visually disabled have been assessed in greater detail (Royal National Institute for the Blind).

In order to study the expenditure patterns of disabled people in greater detail a further study has been undertaken in conjunction with the regular Family Expenditure Survey (FES) carried out by OPCS. For a year from July 1986 to June 1987 members of households participating in the FES were screened for disability and those identified as disabled were asked the same questions about their disabilities as on the main survey. Social Research Branch of DHSS are undertaking analysis of the data to compare the financial circumstances of households with and without a disabled member.

1.4 Timetable
To carry out such an extensive programme of research a considerable amount of feasibility and pilot work was

required. The general strategy was first to design and develop the methods required for the survey of disabled adults living in private households and then to modify and extend them as necessary for the other surveys. Once proposals and preliminary questionnaires had been developed a major consultation exercise took place. Comments were sought from over 150 different organisations and individuals, including both the main voluntary organisations and leading academics and professionals in the disability field. Following this, final proposals were agreed with DHSS. Figure 1 summarises the timetable for the whole programme of research.

1.5 Coverage of the surveys
The results presented in this report relate only to disabled adults; those for children will be given in a later report (see below for details of reports). The people included and the questions asked of them on the surveys of disabled adults living in private households and communal establishments are described here, while the corresponding description of the children's surveys will be included in the relevant report.

1.5.1 Adults living in private households
The main interview with disabled adults comprised predetermined questions. The first part asked questions about the nature of the disabilities experienced by the subject of the interview. The answers to this part of the interview were used to assess the type and severity of disability. The second part covered the circumstances of

the disabled person and aimed to examine the consequences of disability in a number of different areas.

(a) The 'assessment of disability' questions
Before asking in detail about disabilities, some questions were included to establish the nature of the complaints giving rise to disabilities. Then questions about each disability established whether it was sufficiently severe for the subject to be eligible for a full interview and for more detailed questions to be asked. The further questions about each area of disability provided information about the nature and level of severity of the disability.

The questions on disabilities and health problems were covered in the following sections:

  A Walking
  B Steps and stairs
  C Bending and straightening
  D Falling and balance
  E Reaching and stretching
  F Holding, gripping and turning
  G Seeing (at a distance and to read)
  H Hearing
  J Noises in the head or ears
  K Control of bladder and bowels
  L Fits and convulsions
  M Being understood and understanding others
  N Social behaviour and intellectual functioning
  P Other problems that limit daily activities:
     —breathlessness, wheezing and coughing
     —difficulties with eating, drinking and digestion
     —severe pain or irritation
     —disfigurement or deformities
  R Difficulties with self-care and household activities

In addition some questions about dependence on others for help with self-care activities were included which were not intended as part of the assessment of disability. Questions were also asked about the people who provided this sort of care.

(b) The 'circumstances of the disabled' questions
Although concentrating particularly on the financial circumstances of the disabled person and the extra expenses of disability, this part also covered a number of other topics. It was divided into the following sections:

  S Health and social services
  T Aids and adaptations
  U Extra personal costs
  V Mobility and transport
  W Education and employment
  X Income
  Y Household finances
  Z Financial situation

1.5.2 Adults living in communal establishments
The interview was a shortened and simplified version of that used for the private household survey. The main reasons for adaptations to the questions were:

(i) Preliminary analysis of information from the private household survey indicated the key questions required to assess severity of disability. Redundant questions could therefore be omitted.

(ii) The piloting of the private household schedules in communal establishments showed that some questions were inappropriate outside the private household setting, for example, those on independence in certain daily activities.

(iii) A substantial proportion of interviews could not be carried out with disabled people themselves and detailed information about a disabled adult living in a communal establishment was not always available from the person being interviewed. Questions about attitudes could not be asked and those dealing with the frequency of an event or about financial circumstances were particularly difficult. Even when residents were interviewed in person, many were elderly and frail, or indeed very ill, and were easily tired, which limited the type and number of questions that could be asked.

Other main differences in the coverage of the two surveys were that the survey in communal establishments asked only about the use of and not about the need for services, and questions on finances concentrated on the management of the resident's affairs rather than asking about income and expenditure.

1.6 Coverage of this report
The main purpose of this report is to present estimates of the prevalence of disability among adults in Great Britain, according to severity. In order to interpret these results it is necessary to have some understanding of the conceptual approach and the methods adopted for this study, an account of which is given in Chapter 2. The main results are then presented in Chapters 3 and 4. These chapters also contain some descriptive information about the characteristics of disabled adults on both surveys. Not only is this of interest in its own right, but it also gives some idea of the size of the main subgroups that will be available for the more detailed investigation of the consequences of disability covered in later reports.

Chapters 5 to 8 describe in more detail the methods used on these surveys. Chapter 5 covers the design of the private household survey, including the screening procedures which also identified the sample of disabled children living in private households. Chapter 6 describes the design of the communal establishment survey. Chapter 7 explains how the definition of disability and measures of severity were developed for the study and Chapter 8 gives details of the procedures used to derive national estimates from the survey results.

1.7 Note on terminology
In recent years views have been expressed about the terms that should be used to describe the people who are the subject of this study. Some people prefer to speak

of 'people with disabilities' rather than 'disabled people' to avoid any suggestions of labelling. However, in reports of this nature the term chosen will be used frequently and so for brevity we refer to 'disabled people'.

The term 'communal establishments' is used to refer to places other than private households in which disabled people live. Chapter 6 describes in detail what sort of places these were and mentions some that were not covered by the survey. Again in the interest of brevity, the term 'establishments' has sometimes been used, particularly on tables. It should be taken to have the same meaning as 'communal establishments' whenever it is used.

1.8 Plans for later reports on the study

Because of the wide coverage of the programme of research and the sequential timetables for the four surveys, it is intended to produce a series of reports on different topics of which this is the first. This means that the early reports can be produced before all the survey analysis is complete and those who are interested in specific topics can refer to the relevant report. The reports will be published under the general title *OPCS Surveys of Disability in Great Britain*.

2 Concepts and methods in the assessment of disability

2.1 Introduction

A primary aim of the study was to provide estimates of the number of people in Great Britain with different levels of severity of disability. In designing a programme of research to provide this information, three key issues were addressed:

(i) what was meant by disability, both in conceptual and operational terms;

(ii) how people with disabilities were to be identified, and

(iii) how severity of disability was to be measured.

This chapter is concerned particularly with the first of these issues, as it is essential to the interpretation of the results presented in Chapters 3 and 4. A brief summary is given here of how people with disabilities were identified and how severity has been measured, but a full account of these is left until later chapters. Chapters 5 and 6 describe how disabled people were identified for the surveys in private households and communal establishments respectively. Chapter 7 describes how severity of disability has been measured and Chapter 8 describes the means by which national estimates are derived from the survey results.

2.2 Concepts and definitions

Estimates of the prevalence of disability derived from any study depend on the choice of concepts and the methods used. These in turn depend on the particular purposes and aims of the study in question. This point is worth emphasising because it means that estimates from this study will not necessarily be comparable with those obtained from others using different concepts or methods, and the methods developed for this study cannot be used for other purposes without further development and validation.

Another very important determinant of prevalence rates is the threshold of severity which is chosen to decide whether or not someone should be included in a particular study.

2.2.1 Disability as a continuum

It is misleading to think of people as either disabled or not disabled. As soon as one tries to define 'disabled' in terms that can be used on a survey it becomes apparent that there is a wide variety of possible definitions and large numbers of people could be included or excluded depending on which was used. It is more helpful to think of disability as a *continuum* ranging from very severe to slight disability. This idea can be applied both to individual disabilities and to the concept of overall disability, which is the overall degree of limitation resulting from the separate effects of individual disabilities. The definition of disability for a particular survey is determined by where on the continuum a threshold level is set above which people are included in the survey estimates. This is illustrated in Figure 2.1.

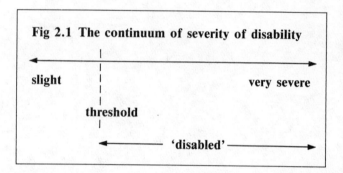

Fig 2.1 The continuum of severity of disability

slight   very severe

threshold

'disabled'

Estimates of the overall prevalence of disability are based on the number of people found to have disabilities above the threshold level. On this basis it makes no sense to say that a particular survey under- or over-estimates the *absolute* prevalence of disability (unless the methods used to identify people with disabilities were inadequate), since there is no *absolute* prevalence; prevalence depends on how disability has been defined and measured on the survey in question.

The level of disability chosen as the threshold for inclusion on a particular survey will depend on the aims of the survey. DHSS told us that previous experience had shown that there was a need for information about the financial circumstances and possible need for services of people at lower levels of disability than were included in the 1969 survey. Clearly this will produce higher prevalence estimates, but it does not imply that there are more disabled people now than in 1969. The choice of a relatively low threshold of disability means that it is all the more important to avoid any sweeping conclusions—for instance that all those included in this study are unable to support themselves, or are unable to lead normal lives or are necessarily dependent on services or social security benefits.

Prevalence estimates will also depend on the types of disability studied, as well as the threshold of severity. This study includes all types of disability, whereas many surveys are concerned only with disabilities with a physical origin.

2.2.2 Methods of assessment

Methods of assessment used on surveys to provide population estimates differ substantially from those used in judicial and clinical decisions, for example for benefits, compensation and the provision of services. This is because the methods used for assessing individuals are rarely the same as those used to classify populations. In the case of the former, detailed and time-consuming assessments by professionals such as doctors can be justified on the grounds that the methods are sensitive to individual circumstances and produce results which are equitable between individuals. On surveys, however, provided the methods used deal adequately with the majority of people in the survey, it does not matter if a small minority would have been classified differently had more detailed procedures been used. There are many sources of error in sample surveys, of which this kind of measurement error is only one. The standard approach used on disability surveys is for trained interviewers to collect information systematically from individuals about their limitations which is then summarised in a standard way to arrive at an overall measure for each individual on the survey.

2.2.3 ICIDH concepts and definitions

A major problem in the general field of disability lies in the confusion over terminology. Legislation, administration, academic research and everyday speech alike use terms inconsistently; the same terms are used to refer to different concepts and different terms are used to refer to identical concepts. Fortunately a way out of the confusion is proposed in the International Classification of Impairments Disabilities and Handicaps (ICIDH). This World Health Organisation classification produced by Phillip Wood provides comprehensive definitions of the main concepts in this area and it is these definitions that have been adopted for this study.

The ICIDH identifies three different concepts as consequences of disease and presents a classification for each. They are defined as follows:

Impairment
'Any loss or abnormality of psychological, physiological or anatomical structure or function.' Here we are dealing with parts or systems of the body that do not work.

Disability
'Any restriction or lack (resulting from an impairment) of ability to perform an activity in the manner or within the range considered normal for a human being.' Here we are talking about things people cannot do.

Handicap
'A disadvantage for a given individual, resulting from an impairment or disability, that limits or prevents the fulfilment of a role (depending on age, sex and social and cultural factors) for that individual.' This is in relation to a particular environment and relationships with other people.

The ICIDH uses the term 'disablement' to refer to all the consequences of disease, that is it embraces all three concepts. It includes a detailed classification for each of the three concepts, designed to allow coding from individual case records.

The relationship between the concepts can be represented as:

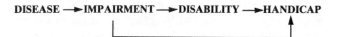

DISEASE ⟶ IMPAIRMENT ⟶ DISABILITY ⟶ HANDICAP

The following examples illustrate the relationship between the three concepts:

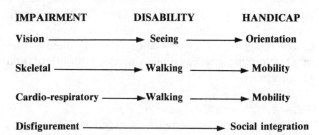

IMPAIRMENT	DISABILITY	HANDICAP
Vision	⟶ Seeing	⟶ Orientation
Skeletal	⟶ Walking	⟶ Mobility
Cardio-respiratory	⟶ Walking	⟶ Mobility
Disfigurement		⟶ Social integration

In the case of some impairments, such as vision and hearing, there is a more or less one-to-one correspondence between impairment and disability if the impairment is sufficiently serious. However, it should be noted that although a large proportion of the population suffer from visual impairment, because of the availability of adequate glasses or contact lenses to correct impaired vision, far fewer people can be said to have a seeing disability. In other cases, as in two of the examples shown above, different impairments can give rise to the same disability. Conversely, one impairment may result in more than one disability; for example, severe intellectual impairment might result in a variety of different disabilities. The lack of correspondence between disabilities and handicaps is even more apparent than between impairments and disabilities, as handicaps are affected by such things as differences in the environment, the availability of others to help and the roles an individual is expected to fulfil. Sometimes an impairment results in a handicap without any disability, as in the case of disfigurement shown above.

It is important to keep these concepts clear because they are often used with different meanings. People frequently have rather stereotyped views of what is meant by disability and who 'the disabled' are, imagining perhaps a young person in a wheelchair or a child with Down's syndrome. Elderly people in general are not usually thought of as being disabled, but the above definition of disability means that it is the old who are most likely to be disabled as the aging process takes its toll and restricts the activities that the elderly can perform. As we shall see, among the very elderly 'disability', in the sense of some restriction on activity, can be said to be the norm.

Another problem is that people tend to use all the disability-related concepts interchangeably or inconsistently, partly reflecting common usage in particular situations. For example, everyday speech refers to people with 'mental handicaps'. According to the ICIDH terminology, this should be 'mental impairments' because the terms 'physical', 'mental' and 'sensory' are correctly applied to impairments rather than to disabilities. A classification of types of disabilities will therefore be in terms of activities in which performance is limited rather than the impairments or complaints causing the limitations.

Yet another problem with classifications applied to individuals on surveys is that, whichever concept is used, many people will have more than one impairment/disability/handicap and so cannot be assigned uniquely to one category comprising all those with a particular type. For example, since multiple health problems become more common with advancing years, elderly people may well have physical, mental and sensory impairments causing a variety of disabilities and handicaps.

2.2.4 Social Security concepts
The key concept underlying assessments for several social security benefits paid to the disabled, notably industrial injuries benefits and severe disablement allowance, is 'loss of faculty', which is roughly equivalent to 'impairment' defined above. The terms 'disability' and 'disablement' are also used in connection with the administration of these benefits, but with different definitions which are given below:

Loss of faculty
'Any pathological condition or any loss (including a reduction) of the normal physical or mental function of some organ or part of the body . . . including disfigurement.'

Disability
'Inability to do things or do them equally as well as a person of the same age and sex whose physical and mental condition is normal, which arises from a loss of faculty.'

Disablement
'The overall effect of the relevant disabilities, ie the overall inability to perform the normal activities of life—the loss of health, strength and power to enjoy a normal life.'

The main difference in the definition of disability given here, compared with the ICIDH definition given above, is that it includes a reference to what is considered normal for someone of the same age and sex. The concepts of disablement are also different; the social security concept seems somewhat similar to the ICIDH concept of handicap, although it does not specifically mention disadvantage.

In connection with benefit entitlement disablement is measured on a percentage scale. To be eligible for severe disablement allowance an assessment of at least 80% disablement is required (among other criteria), while for industrial injuries benefit the amount of payment varies with the percentage assessment. An assessment of 100% disablement means that someone is entitled to the maximum benefit rather than being literally totally disabled.

2.3 Choice of concept for the current study
We began by looking at a method of assessment for the study based on the 'loss of faculty' approach. However, the benefits based on this concept require a medical examination to assess the degree of loss of faculty and the resulting disablement. This is obviously necessary in the case of industrial injuries benefit because the loss of faculty attributable to the industrial accident or disease has to be assessed separately from any loss of faculty arising from other causes, such as other injury or disease or the general effects of aging. It is for this reason that a reference to what is normal for someone of the same age and sex is included. Above a minimum level, loss of faculty due to an industrial accident or disease will result in the payment of some benefit, even if the resulting disability is slight. This is specifically intended to compensate someone for suffering a loss of faculty attributable to their occupation.

When considering a method of assessing disability in general, whatever its cause, there seems less justification for adopting this approach. If all disability is to be assessed, there is no logical reason for starting from impairment or loss of faculty. The concept of compensation does not seem relevant and reference to what is normal for someone of a particular age becomes difficult to operate in relation to elderly people and also seems inappropriate; what is expected of a normal eighty-year-old? Is it reasonable to expect a certain amount of disability as a natural consequence of aging and effectively disregard it for assessment purposes? We have taken the view that limitations arising from aging are properly considered as disabilities and so an age-related criterion is inappropriate. This view follows the ICIDH definition of disability.

Apart from there being no obvious logical reason for starting from the concept of impairment or loss of faculty, a number of practical problems arose when attempts were made in early work on the study to start from this basis.

First, disabled people themselves and organisations representing their interests generally found questions about disability easier to answer and more relevant than questions about impairment. The general reaction during preliminary trials was that people could not see the point of being asked questions about impairments unless they resulted in disability and then it was the disability (or handicap) that resulted that they really wanted to talk about. Impairments which were apparent to the interviewer would not necessarily be mentioned if they were not thought to affect the informant's daily life to any extent.

Second, assessments of impairment would require clinical examination, tests and judgements. It was not considered feasible to arrange for all subjects to be medically examined; the study required an approach which would be suitable for interviewers to operate as part of a standard survey interview.

It was therefore decided that the study would identify people with disabilities by asking directly about disabilities and would not cover impairments (except when thought necessary to ensure that people with disabilities such as those caused by mental or psychological problems were not missed).

2.3.1 Disabilities covered by the study

The study aimed to cover, as far as possible, all the areas of disability included in the ICIDH. Disabilities were classified along the lines of the ICIDH, but with some differences where the ICIDH was considered to be either too detailed or not detailed enough for the purpose of this study. Questions were then devised to identify people with a disability in each of the areas. It was necessary to decide the form in which questions should be asked, and in particular whether to ask about what people *can* do or what they *do* do, that is between what they are thought capable of and their actual performance. It was decided that the former was more appropriate, on the grounds that benefit assessment is made on this basis and the main focus of the study was on social security interests.

The main concept used in this study and the basis of the estimates is disability, but the study has also been designed to provide some information about the extent of handicap resulting from disability. The focus is on the financial consequences of disability, but various other aspects of handicap, notably financial and occupational handicaps, have been covered on the different surveys, although necessarily not in very much detail.

Although it was decided not to assess impairment comprehensively, some questions about impairments were included. According to the ICIDH, pain and suffering generally are seen as consequences of disease or disorder which may lead to activity limitations and are therefore viewed as impairments. On the survey of adults living in private households, where most disabled adults were interviewed in person, questions could be asked about subjective feelings and sensations, and so questions designed to assess pain, anxiety and depression were included. However, they do not contribute to the assessment of disability, except in so far as they act to reduce capacity to carry out a particular activity.

2.4 Identification of people with disabilities

2.4.1 The private household surveys

There is no comprehensive list of all disabled people in the country from which a sample for the surveys could be drawn. In order to identify samples of people with disabilities living in private households for interview it was necessary to screen a large sample of the general population. The basic method was a series of screening procedures which aimed to move successively towards the identification of the group of interest, without excluding people inadvertently.

Initially a large sample of the general population (100,000 addresses) was screened to identify people with some form of disability. This was done by asking the occupiers of the address to complete a short questionnaire which asked about problems with a number of different daily activities. Anyone with any of these problems was potentially available for the next stage of the survey.

At the second stage interviewers approached all those aged under 60 and half of those aged 60 or over who had been screened in at the first stage as having at least one problem. Disability is much more common among older people and so almost twice as many disabled people aged 60 or over as opposed to under 60 were identified. Interviewing only half of those aged 60 or over meant that roughly equal numbers of people in the two age bands were interviewed, giving scope for similar detail of analysis without incurring the extra costs of interviewing all those aged 60 or over. Results in this report have been weighted to restore the two age bands to their correct proportions.

In theory it would be possible to design a set of screening questions covering all types of disabilities which identified people with equivalent levels of severity regardless of which disabilities they might have and which could be answered accurately so that all those with a particular level of disability were identified and none were missed.

In practice it was possible neither to design a set of questions that identified people at the same level of disability regardless of type, nor to ensure that people always answered the screening questions accurately.

The screening questions were therefore designed to screen in people at a somewhat lower level of severity than required eventually, in order not to risk excluding anyone who might be of interest, and a second screening stage was used at the start of the main interviews to check answers given at the first stage and to determine whether the individual was sufficiently disabled to be included on the survey.

Although this procedure reduces the risk of missing people who in fact should have been included as being sufficiently disabled, it cannot ensure that no one is missed. It is always possible that some people with disabilities chose not to reveal them in answer to the screening questions and of course some did not respond to the screening questionnaire at all.

The first step in defining the threshold level for this study lay in the choice of screening questions used at the initial stage, since only people who responded positively to at least one question were included in later stages of the study. These questions were chosen to include people with disabilities that were likely to have a significant effect on the ability to carry out normal everyday activities. The choice of questions requires judgements to be made, and we were guided by the sort of questions that have commonly been used in other studies of disability and by discussions and consultation with experts in disability research and organisations representing disabled people.

Despite the use of a threshold level, it is likely that some people who receive services or who use aids or appliances will not have been included in the study. This is a consequence of the choice of disability as the basis of the study. Some people with impairments may as a result of the use of aids or appliances have only a very minor level of disability and as such fall below the threshold level. Clearly millions of people with sight impairments which are overcome by the use of glasses would not be considered as disabled, but equally someone with a cardiac pacemaker that allowed them to carry out normal everyday activities without any problems would not be considered disabled for the purposes of the survey. Similarly someone with an impairment which could be overcome by taking regular medication and which did not affect their everyday activities would not be included on the survey.

It was only possible to establish the level of severity at which the screening questions were in fact operating once a measure of severity common to all types of disability had been developed, which was not produced until after the interviews had taken place. This meant that some people were interviewed in full who were subsequently excluded because they fell below the threshold eventually used on the survey.

Figure 2.2 illustrates the successive screening stages used to identify people along the disability continuum. The total population is represented as a triangle, since relatively few people are very severely disabled, and the numbers increase as one goes along the continuum towards the more minor disabilities.

2.4.2 The communal establishments surveys

Preliminary work was undertaken to draw up lists of institutions to be covered by the surveys. For the survey of disabled adults a screening stage was carried out to identify those establishments that catered for permanent residents, as opposed to those having only temporary residents. Temporary residents would have had the chance of being included in the private household survey at their permanent address. In the corresponding children's survey all establishments providing residential accommodation for children were screened to identify those which catered for disabled children who were long term residents.

All permanently resident adults living in communal establishments were assumed to have some degree of

disability and so an initial screening stage to identify those with disabilities, as on the private household survey, was felt to be unnecessary. In the case of children, a further screening stage took place when interviewers visited the selected establishments to identify individual children who were both long term residents and who had a disability.

2.5 Measuring severity of disability

It was decided to construct a measure of severity of disability specially for this study, as existing scales were considered unsuitable for a variety of reasons described in Chapter 7. Severity of disability was defined as the extent to which an individual's performance of activities is limited by impairments. The survey collected information about limitations in performing particular activities, but provided no means of obtaining a measure of the overall effect of all limitations taken together. In order to compare disabilities and to combine information about different disabilities into an overall measure a criterion of overall severity was required. It was decided to use people's judgements of the relative severity of different disabilities separately and in combination as the criterion. This moves the criterion in the direction of handicap rather than disability, because people are required to judge the likely effect of particular disabilities on someone's daily life. However, the judgements were not made in relation to any specific set of circumstances or for particular characteristics of individuals (such as age or sex), and were not designed to measure handicap as defined by the ICIDH.

A set of exercises were designed to obtain such judgements in a systematic way. The criterion of overall severity is therefore based on a consensus of assessments of people acting as 'judges' and as such is subjective, but it is by no means arbitrary; the judges were given careful instructions and a high level of agreement in their assessments was achieved.

Before the judgements were obtained preliminary statistical analysis was carried out to explore relationships between different disabilities and to develop scales in ten main areas of disability:

Locomotion
Reaching and stretching
Dexterity
Seeing
Hearing
Personal care
Continence
Communication
Behaviour
Intellectual functioning

The judgements were carried out in three separate stages:

—between disabilities within the ten separate areas
—between disabilities in different areas
—between different combinations of disabilities

Fig 2.2 Successive stages in the identification of people with disabilities

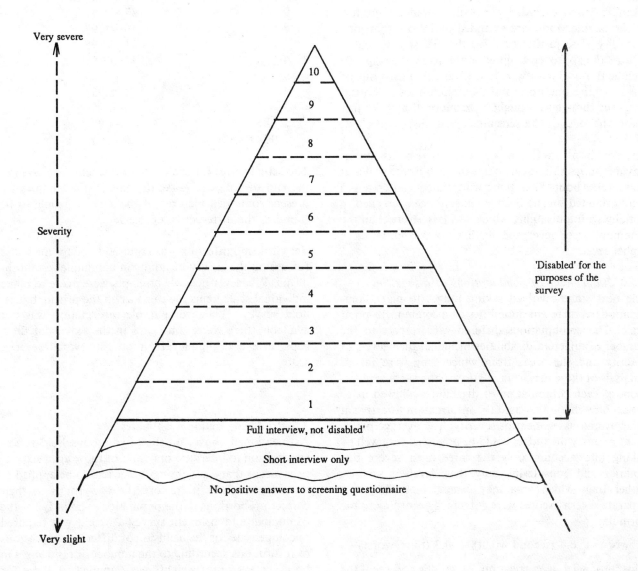

Very severe

Severity

Very slight

10
9
8
7
6
5
4
3
2
1

'Disabled' for the purposes of the survey

Full interview, not 'disabled'

Short interview only

No positive answers to screening questionnaire

The judges included professionals with expertise in disability, people carrying out research on disability including staff from OPCS and DHSS working on the surveys, people with disabilities, those caring for them and people from voluntary organisations concerned with disability. Altogether nearly 100 people took part in one or more of the stages.

2.5.1 Judgements within areas of disability

At this stage judges were given a set of cards describing limitations in the performance of activities in each of the ten areas in turn. They were asked to place them on an 11-point scale to reflect how disabling they thought each was in relation to the others in the same area. No comparisons were made between limitations from different areas. Calculation of the average placement of each card produced a scale of severity of limitation for each area which reflected the consensus of opinion of how severely limiting each activity was.

2.5.2 Judgements between disabilities in different areas

Comparison of the relative degree of limitation of disabilities from different areas was achieved by asking the judges to consider those activities rated most and

least limiting in each area at the previous stage. They were asked to place these on a 15-point scale to reflect their view of how severely limiting each was in relation to all the other activities from the extreme ends of the separate scales. Once the average placements of these end-points from each scale was established it was a simple matter to calculate the position of all the intervening points, preserving the relative distances from the previous stage. Thus all disabilities were placed on a common scale and could be compared in terms of their relative severity.

2.5.3 Establishing a common lower level of severity for all areas

It was only at this stage we were able to discover how successful the screening procedures had been at identifying people at the same level of severity regardless of which type of disability they might have. If the screening questions had worked perfectly in this respect the bottom items on each of the scales would have been at the same level of severity on the common scale. Not surprisingly there were differences and so a common lower level of severity was set to apply to all areas of disability. In effect this meant eliminating from consideration those people whose disabilities were all below this level. Thus people with several minor disabilities were excluded, although in practice very few of the people who were excluded had more than one disability. The justification for this decision is that it follows the approach adopted at the screening stage, to include those who answered positively to at least one of the screening questions and to exclude those who did not, even though they might have minor disabilities just below the level of the screening questions.

The common lower level was chosen to be as low as possible subject to having items on each of the scales at that level. About 5% of those who had been interviewed were excluded on the basis of having been screened in initially with a disability which was less severe than the common lower level and having no disabilities at a higher level.

2.5.4 Judgements of combinations of disabilities
The next stage involved asking judges to place combinations of different disabilities on a common 15-point scale. The combinations differed with respect to the number of different disabilities included, their levels of severity and the areas from which they were taken. Analysis of these factors in relation to the average placement of each combination of disabilities allowed us to model how the judges used the information to arrive at their overall assessment of severity. The average placement given by the judges could be predicted very well by taking into account only the three most severe disabilities and considering only their level of severity rather than which area they came from. The three separate severity scores were combined according to the formula:

worst + 0.4 (second worst) + 0.3 (third worst)

This produced a correlation of 96.4% between the ratings predicted by the model and the judges' actual ratings; a very good fit.

2.5.5 The overall severity scale
Applying the above formula to everyone on the survey enabled an overall severity score to be calculated for each person. A few disabilities which were not included in the ten areas listed above were incorporated into the final score, as described in Chapter 7. The scores were grouped into ten severity categories. The advantage of having ten, rather than fewer categories, is that when numbers permit the full set can be used, or adjacent categories can be combined to give five, which is still sufficient for examining trends associated with severity.

It is worth noting that since the highest score on a single scale is 13, all those with scores higher than this must have more than one disability.

Severity category	Overall severity score
10 (most severe)	19 or higher
9	17–18.95
8	15–16.95
7	13–14.95
6	11–12.95
5	9–10.95
4	7–8.95
3	5–6.95
2	3–4.95
1 (least severe)	0.5–2.95

The actual scales for each area of disability are given at the end of Chapter 7. At the end of this chapter we present some pen pictures of the sort of people to be found in the different categories.

Very little modification was required to adapt the scales for use on the survey of adults in communal establishments. Whenever possible attempts were made to make individual scale items the same as on the private household survey. When comparable information was not available there were some gaps in the scale, but these gaps have a negligible effect on the overall severity score.

2.6 Producing national estimates
As mentioned above, on the private household survey the decision to interview only half of those aged sixty or over meant that a weighting factor had to be applied to the survey results to restore the age-groups to their correct proportions in the population. Similarly for the communal establishment survey a weight was required to compensate for the inclusion of different proportions of institutions according to the number of residents. On both surveys other weights were applied to allow for non-response at various stages and to bring the sample survey estimates up to population estimates, as described in Chapter 8.

Results are presented in several different ways: as population totals in thousands, as prevalence rates in terms of the number of disabled people per thousand of the population and as percentages of those interviewed (and defined as disabled) on the surveys. In the last case the base numbers on which the percentages were calculated have been set to a total of 10,000 for the private household survey and 4,000 for the communal establishment survey, roughly reflecting the actual number of interviews on each. However, individual cases have been weighted to allow for different sampling probabilities and non-response, as mentioned above, and so as far as possible the results give a true picture of the population distributions.

'Pen pictures' of typical cases in each severity category

Notes

1. All the disabilities mentioned on the questionnaires are listed. Thus if a disability area is not mentioned the individual does not have a problem in that area.

2. The disability areas are shown in order of their severity scores. Only the three highest contribute to the overall severity score.

3. Information on complaints causing disabilities is given when available. However, not everyone gave information about complaints causing their disabilities; cases 1.2 and 2.1 recorded no information relating to the disabilities mentioned.

Severity category 1

Case 1.1
  Man aged 59
  Deaf in one ear
  Overall severity score 1.5

Hearing score 1.5

Difficulty hearing someone talking in a normal voice in a quiet room

Case 1.2
  Man aged 50
  Overall severity score 1.7

Seeing score 1.5

Cannot see well enough to recognise a friend across the road
Has difficulty seeing to read ordinary newspaper print

Hearing score 0.5

Difficulty following a conversation against background noise

Severity category 2

Case 2.1
  Man aged 75
  Overall severity score 4.25

Intellectual functioning score 3.5

Often forgets what was supposed to be doing in the middle of something
Often loses track of what's being said in the middle of a conversation
Often forgets to turn things off such as fires, cookers or taps

Behaviour score 1.5

Sometimes sits for hours doing nothing
Finds it difficult to stir himself to do things

Hearing score 0.5

Has difficulty following a conversation against background noise

Case 2.2
  Woman aged 71
  Angina
  Eye problem
  Overall severity score 4.25

Locomotion score 3.0

Cannot walk 200 yards without stopping or severe discomfort

Seeing score 1.5

Cannot see well enough to recognise a friend across the road
Has difficulty seeing to read ordinary newspaper print

Severity category 3

Case 3.1
  Woman aged 31
  High tone deafness in both ears
  Overall severity score 6.05

Communication score 5.5

Finds it quite difficult to understand people who know her well
Finds it very difficult to understand strangers

Intellectual functioning score 1.0

Often loses track of what's being said in the middle of a conversation

Hearing score 0.5

Difficulty following a conversation against background noise

Case 3.2
  Man aged 47
  Spinal arthritis
  Overall severity score 5.85

Reaching and stretching score 4.5

Has difficulty putting either hand behind back to put jacket on or tuck shirt in

Locomotion score 3.0

Cannot walk 200 yards without stopping or severe discomfort
Can only walk up and down a flight of 12 stairs if holds on (doesn't need a rest)

Personal care score 1.0

Has difficulty getting in and out of bed

Hearing score 0.5

Has difficulty following a conversation against background noise

Severity category 4

Case 4.1
  Man 47
  Lumbar spondilysis
  Cervical spondilysis
  Spinal arthritis
  Overall severity score 7.9

Locomotion score 7.5

Has fallen 12 or more times in the last year
Cannot bend down and pick up something from the floor and straighten up again
Can only walk up and down a flight of 12 stairs if holds on (doesn't need a rest)
Cannot walk 200 yards without stopping or severe discomfort

Personal care score 1.0

Has difficulty getting in and out of bed

Hearing score 0.5

Has difficulty following a conversation against background noise

Case 4.2
  Man aged 25
  Deaf in both ears
  Overall severity score 7.7

Hearing score 5.5

Cannot hear a doorbell, alarm clock or telephone bell
Cannot use the telephone
Cannot follow a TV programme at a volume others find acceptable
Has difficulty hearing someone talking in a normal voice in a quiet room

Communication score 5.5

Finds it very difficult to understand strangers

Severity category 5

Case 5.1
  Woman aged 75
  Phlebitis
  Overall severity score 10.2

Continence score 8.0

Loses control of bladder at least once every 24 hours

Locomotion score 5.5

Cannot walk 50 yards without stopping or severe discomfort
Can only walk up and down a flight of 12 stairs if holds on (doesn't need a rest)

Case 5.2
Woman aged 16
Mild cerebral palsy
One leg ¼" shorter than other
Overall severity score 10

Intellectual functioning 6.0

Often gets confused about what time of day it is
Cannot read a short article in a newspaper
Cannot count well enough to handle money
Cannot watch a half hour TV programme all the way through and tell someone what it was about
Thoughts tend to be muddled or slow

Communication score 5.5

Finds it very difficult to understand strangers

Locomotion score 1.5

Can only walk up and down a flight of stairs if goes sideways or one step at a time

Severity category 6
Case 6.1
Man aged 65
Arthritis in spine and legs
Stroke affecting right side
Heart condition
Overall severity score 11.55

Locomotion score 7.0

Always needs to hold on to something to keep balance
Cannot bend down and pick up something from the floor and straighten up again
Can only walk up and down a flight of 12 stairs if holds on and takes a rest
Cannot walk 200 yards without stopping or severe discomfort

Reaching and stretching score 6.5

Has difficulty holding either arm in front to shake hands with someone

Dexterity score 6.5

Has difficulty picking up and pouring from a full kettle or serving food from a pan using a spoon or ladle
Has difficulty unscrewing the lid of a coffee jar or using a pen or pencil
Can pick up a small object such as a safety pin with one hand but not the other

Case 6.2
Woman aged 40
Epileptic
Overall severity score 12.9

Consciousness score 8.0

Has fits once a year but less than 4 times a year
Has fits during the daytime

Intellectual functioning score 7.0

Cannot count well enough to handle money
Cannot write a short letter to someone without help
Cannot read a short article in a newspaper
Cannot watch a half hour TV programme all the way through and tell someone what it was about
Thoughts tend to be muddled or slow
Often gets confused about what time of day it is

Behaviour score 7.0

Feels the need to have someone present all the time
Finds it difficult to stir herself to do things
Sometimes sits for hours doing nothing
Often feels aggressive or hostile towards other people
Finds relationships with people outside the family difficult

Communication score 2.0

Is quite difficult for strangers to understand

Severity category 7
Case 7.1
Man aged 31
Addicted to tablets
Overall severity score 13.9

Behaviour score 10.5

Gets so upset that hits other people
Gets so upset that breaks or rips things up
Feels the need to have someone present all the time

Finds relationships with people outside the family very difficult
Sometimes sits for hours doing nothing

Communication score 8.5

Is impossible for strangers to understand
Is quite difficult for people who know him well to understand

Case 7.2
Man aged 79
Stroke
Overall severity score 14.45

Locomotion score 7.5

Has fallen 12 or more times in the last year
Cannot walk 50 yards without stopping or severe discomfort
Can only walk up and down a flight of 12 stairs if holds on and takes a rest

Dexterity score 6.5

Has difficulty picking up and pouring from a full kettle
Has difficulty using a pen or pencil

Continence score 6.5

Loses control of bowels at least twice a month
Loses control of bladder occasionally

Severity category 8
Case 8.1
Woman 32
Spastic
Overall severity score 16.65

Locomotion score 9.5

Can only walk a few steps without stopping or severe discomfort

Intellectual functioning score 9.5

Often forgets what was supposed to be doing in the middle of something
Often loses track of what's being said in the middle of a conversation
Often forgets to turn things off such as fires, cookers and taps
Often forgets the name of people in the family or friends seen regularly
Often gets confused about what time of day it is
Thoughts tend to be muddled or slow
Cannot write a short letter to someone without help
Cannot count well enough to handle money

Consciousness score 10.0

Has fits during the daytime
Has fits once a month but less than once a week

Seeing score 8.0

Cannot see well enough to recognize a friend who is an arm's length away
Has difficulty seeing to read ordinary newspaper print

Behaviour score 7.5

Gets so upset that breaks and rips things up
Feels the need to have someone present all the time
Often feels aggressive or hostile towards other people

Dexterity score 6.5

Has difficulty picking up and pouring from a full kettle and serving food from a pan using a spoon or ladle
Has difficulty wringing out light washing and using a pair of scissors
Cannot pick up and carry a 5 lb bag of potatoes with either hand

Case 8.2
Woman 77
'Old age'
Overall severity score 15.8

Behaviour score 10.5

Gets so upset that hits other people or injures herself
Finds it difficult to stir herself to do things

Intellectual functioning score 7.0

Often forgets what was supposed to be doing in the middle of something
Often loses track of what's being said in the middle of a conversation
Often forgets the name of people in the family or friends seen regularly
Thoughts tend to be muddled or slow

Cannot watch a half hour TV programme all the way through and tell someone what it was about
Cannot remember and pass on a message correctly

Dexterity score 8.0

Cannot squeeze out the water from a sponge with either hand
Can turn a tap or control knob with one hand but not the other
Has difficulty wringing out light washing or using a pair of scissors

Severity category 9
Case 9.1
Man aged 79
Arthritis of spine
Deafness
Overall severity score 18.35

Communication score 12.0

Finds it impossible to understand people who know him well

Personal care score 9.5

Cannot get in and out of bed without help

Hearing score 8.5

Cannot follow a TV programme with the volume turned up
Has difficulty hearing someone talking in a loud voice in a quiet room
Cannot use the telephone

Continence score 8.0

Loses control of bladder at least once every 24 hours

Dexterity score 6.5

Has difficulty serving food from a pan using a spoon or ladle
Has difficulty unscrewing the lid of a coffee jar

Locomotion score 4.5

Cannot bend down far enough to touch knees and straighten up again
Can only walk up and down a flight of 12 stairs if holds on and takes a rest

Seeing score 0.5

Has difficulty seeing to read ordinary newspaper print

Case 9.2
Man aged 30
Mentally retarded
Overall severity score 17.55

Dexterity score 10.5

Cannot pick up and hold a mug of coffee with either hand
Cannot squeeze out water from a sponge with either hand
Has difficulty serving food from a pan using a spoon or ladle
Cannot pick up and carry a 5 lb bag of potatoes with either hand

Behaviour score 10.5

Gets so upset that hits other people or injures himself
Gets so upset that breaks or rips things up
Feels the need to have someone present all the time
Finds relationships with members of the family very difficult

Consciousness score 7.0

Has fits once a year but less than 4 times a year
Loses consciousness during a fit

Locomotion score 6.5

Cannot walk up and down a flight of 12 stairs

Communication score 5.5

Finds it quite difficult to understand people who know him well

Continence score 4.0

Loses control of bowels occasionally

Severity category 10
Case 10.1
Woman 86
Senility
Overall severity score 20.1

Communication score 12.0

Is impossible for people who know her well to understand
Finds it impossible to understand strangers
Finds it quite difficult to understand people who know her well

Intellectual functioning score 12.0

Often forgets what was supposed to be doing in the middle of something
Often loses track of what's being said in the middle of a conversation
Often forgets to turn things off such as fires, cookers and taps
Often forgets the name of people in the family or friends seen regularly
Often gets confused about what time of day it is
Thoughts tend to be muddled or slow
Cannot write a short letter to someone without help
Cannot count well enough to handle money
Cannot watch a half hour TV programme all the way through and tell someone what it was about
Cannot read a short article in a newspaper

Personal care score 11.0

Cannot feed self without help
Cannot also carry out the following without help:
    get in and out of bed
    wash all over
    get in and out of a chair
    wash hands and face
    dress and undress
    get to toilet and use toilet

Locomotion score 9.5

Can only walk a few steps without stopping or severe discomfort
Cannot walk up and down one step

Continence score 8.0

Loses control of bladder at least once every 24 hours
Loses control of bowels at least once a week

Behaviour score 7.5

Gets so upset that breaks or rips things up
Feels the need to have someone present all the time
Sometimes sits for hours doing nothing
Finds it difficult to stir herself to do things

Case 10.2
Man aged 55
Stroke
Overall severity score 19.05

Locomotion score 11.5

Cannot walk at all

Personal care score 11.0

Cannot feed self without help
Cannot also carry out the following without help:
    get in and out of bed
    wash all over
    get in and out of a chair
    wash hands and face
    dress and undress
    get to toilet and use toilet

Dexterity score 10.5

Cannot carry out any activities involving holding, gripping and turning

Reaching and stretching score 9.0

Cannot put either arm up to head to put a hat on
Cannot put either hand behind back to put jacket on or tuck shirt in
Has difficulty holding either arm in front to shake hands with someone

Communication score 5.5

Is very difficult for strangers to understand

Continence score 2.5

Loses control of bladder at least once a month

Seeing 1.5

Cannot see well enough to recognise a friend across the road
Has difficulty seeing to read ordinary newspaper print

15

3 Estimates of the prevalence of disability by severity and type of disability

3.1 Introduction

This chapter presents the main survey estimates of the numbers of disabled adults and the prevalence of disability among adults in Great Britain living both in private households and in communal establishments, by severity and type of disability. Chapter 2 gave a brief account of how the measure of severity was developed. In essence, measures of severity in thirteen different areas of disability were obtained and combined to give an overall measure of severity that has been divided into ten categories of equal width in terms of severity. Category 10 contains the most severely disabled people and category 1 the least severely disabled. More detailed accounts of the development of the measures and the derivation of the estimates are presented in Chapters 7 and 8.

3.2 Estimates of disability by severity

Table 3.1 gives estimates of the number of adults in Great Britain in each of the ten severity categories, in total and separately for the private household and communal establishment populations. Also shown are the 95% confidence intervals, which give an indication of the reliability of the estimates. All estimates derived from sample surveys are subject to sampling error and so a survey estimate will differ from the true population figure. However, there is a 95% probability that the true figure will be within the confidence interval. Thus a survey estimate of 102 with a confidence interval of 17 means that there is a 95% probability that the true estimate lies between 85 and 119. The sizes of the confidence intervals also indicate that it is not appropriate to express estimates of numbers to more than the nearest thousand, nor prevalence rates to more than the nearest whole number per thousand.

The figures from Table 3.1 are illustrated in Figure 3.1 and show that, both overall and among those in private households, there were fewer people in the higher severity categories than in the lower, as might be expected. For example 210 thousand disabled adults were in category 10 compared with just over one million in category 1. But this distribution holds only for the majority who live in private households. Among those living in establishments the reverse is true: over 100 thousand adults were in category 10 and only 13 thousand in category 1. For the most severe level of disability, category 10, similar numbers of people are found in private households and in communal establishments, but below this level the numbers are substantially higher for those in private households. It is clear that substantial proportions of the most severely disabled adults are living in communal establishments, although by no means a large majority.

The shape of the overall distribution emphasises the importance attached to the relative nature of the definition of disability for the purposes of the survey in determining the estimates of total numbers of disabled adults. Changing the definition so that the threshold for disability is somewhat higher would have a dramatic effect on the numbers of people classified as disabled. For example, if those in category 1 were not to be considered disabled, the estimate of the total number of disabled adults would fall by over one million. As Chapter 2 pointed out, different definitions are used for different purposes and on different surveys. A relatively low threshold was chosen for this survey, resulting in high overall estimates.

Table 3.2 presents the numbers from the previous table expressed as rates per thousand of the population, for

Table 3.1   Estimates of numbers of disabled adults in Great Britain by severity category (thousands)

Severity category	In private households		In establishments		Total population	
	Disabled	Confidence interval	Disabled	Confidence interval	Disabled	Confidence interval
	Thousands					
10	102	±17	108	±19	210	±26
9	285	±29	80	±10	365	±31
8	338	±30	58	±9	396	±32
7	447	±35	39	±5	486	±36
6	511	±36	34	±6	545	±36
5	679	±42	29	±4	708	±42
4	676	±40	27	±5	704	±40
3	732	±46	19	±3	750	±46
2	824	±50	16	±3	840	±50
1	1,186	±59	13	±5	1,198	±59
Total	5,780	±161	422	±49	6,202	±169

Fig 3.1 Estimates of numbers of disabled adults in Great Britain by severity category

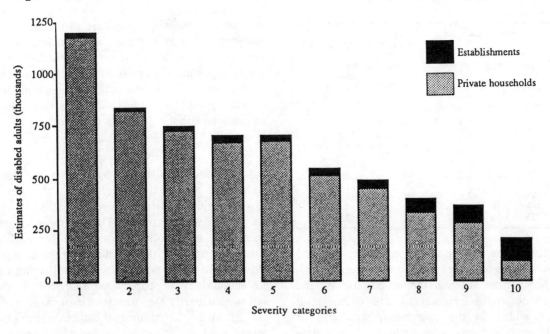

Fig 3.2 Prevalence of disability among adults in Great Britain by severity category

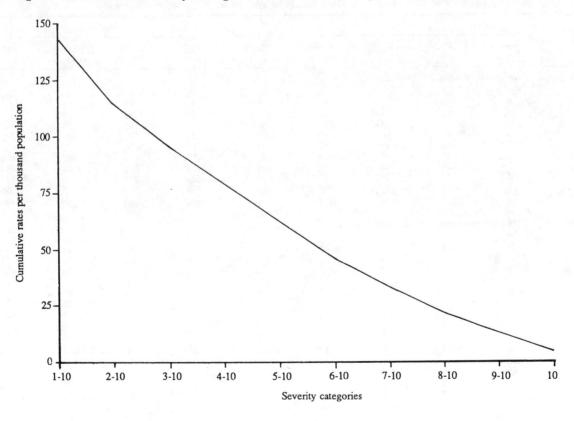

Table 3.2 Prevalence of disability among adults in Great Britain by severity category (cumulative rate per thousand population)

Severity category	In private households		Total (including establishments)	
	Prevalence of disability	Confidence interval	Prevalence of disability	Confidence interval
	Cumulative rate per thousand			
10	2	±0.4	5	±0.6
9–10	9	±0.8	13	±1.0
8–10	17	±1.0	22	±1.3
7–10	27	±1.3	33	±1.6
6–10	39	±1.7	46	±1.9
5–10	55	±2.1	62	±2.3
4–10	71	±2.4	78	±2.6
3–10	88	±2.8	95	±3.0
2–10	107	±3.2	114	±3.4
1–10	135	±3.8	142	±3.9

both the private household population and for the total population. Prevalence rates for the communal establishment population are not shown because of the difficulty of obtaining accurate estimates of the total number of adults in the population who live in communal establishments from which to calculate prevalence rates. This problem is discussed in greater detail in Chapter 8. Table 3.2 shows cumulative rates for each severity band; each line shows the rate per thousand of the population having each level of severity or higher. As in the previous table, the 95% confidence intervals for the estimates are also shown as indicators of reliability.

The results from Table 3.2 for the total population are illustrated in Figure 3.2. They show that five adults per thousand of the population are in the highest severity category, 10, but 142 per thousand have a disability such as to be classified as disabled for the purposes of the survey, that is they fall in category 1 or higher. Put another way, this means that the threshold chosen for the survey has resulted in 14.2% of adults being defined as disabled for the purposes of the survey.

3.3 Estimates of disability by severity and age
Table 3.3 shows the estimates of the numbers of disabled adults in different severity categories separately for different age-groups. The numbers increase with increasing age, both in total and for each severity category up to age 70–79. Thereafter the numbers in the private household population fall, reflecting partly the lower numbers of people aged 80 or over in the population and partly the appearance of large numbers of this group in the communal establishment population where numbers increase dramatically among the very elderly.

Table 3.4 expresses these figures as rates per thousand of the population. It is then clear that although the absolute numbers fall, among the very elderly the rates per thousand of the population continue to rise with age. The relationship with age can be seen clearly in

Table 3.3 Estimates of the number of disabled adults in Great Britain by age and severity category (thousands)

Severity category	Age-group								
	16–19	20–29	30–39	40–49	50–59	60–69	70–79	80 and over	Total
	In private households (thousands)								
10	5	6	4	4	7	15	23	39	102
9	6	10	9	13	28	57	68	93	285
8	5	15	19	24	38	59	92	87	338
7	6	19	24	33	48	78	115	123	447
6	9	30	30	41	60	85	149	107	511
5	12	30	41	50	92	146	176	132	679
4	7	36	46	57	95	152	179	105	676
3	5	28	44	51	109	173	212	109	732
2	4	27	31	57	111	225	263	105	824
1	15	45	77	106	186	308	310	138	1,186
Total	75	245	324	437	774	1,298	1,589	1,037	5,780
	In communal establishments (thousands)								
10	0	7	5	3	4	7	24	58	108
9	0	3	2	2	3	7	18	45	80
8	0	3	3	2	2	5	12	30	58
7	–	1	2	2	1	3	9	22	39
6	–	1	1	2	1	2	9	18	34
5	0	1	1	1	3	2	6	15	29
4	0	1	1	2	1	3	8	12	27
3	–	0	1	1	1	2	6	8	19
2	–	1	0	1	1	2	5	6	16
1	0	0	1	1	1	3	3	3	13
Total	1	19	18	16	19	36	98	217	422
	Total population (thousands)								
10	5	13	9	7	11	22	47	97	210
9	6	13	11	15	31	64	86	138	365
8	5	18	22	26	40	64	104	117	396
7	6	20	26	35	49	81	124	145	486
6	9	31	31	43	61	87	158	125	545
5	12	31	42	51	95	148	182	147	708
4	7	37	47	59	96	155	187	117	704
3	5	28	45	52	110	175	218	117	750
2	4	28	31	58	112	227	268	111	840
1	15	45	78	107	187	311	313	141	1,198
Total	76	264	342	453	793	1,334	1,687	1,254	6,202

Table 3.4 Estimates of prevalence of disability among adults in Great Britain by age and severity category (cumulative rate per thousand population)

Severity category	Age-group								Total
	16–19	20–29	30–39	40–49	50–59	60–69	70–79	80 and over	
In private households (cumulative rate per thousand)									
10	1	1	1	1	1	3	6	25	2
9–10	3	2	2	3	6	13	23	85	9
8–10	5	4	4	6	12	24	46	142	17
7–10	6	6	7	12	21	38	74	222	27
6–10	9	9	11	18	31	53	111	291	39
5–10	12	13	17	26	46	80	155	377	55
4–10	14	17	23	35	62	108	200	445	71
3–10	16	21	28	43	81	139	253	516	88
2–10	17	24	32	52	99	180	318	584	107
1–10	21	29	42	69	131	236	395	674	135
Total population including establishments (cumulative rate per thousand)									
10	1	2	1	1	2	4	11	55	5
9–10	3	3	3	3	7	16	32	133	13
8–10	5	5	5	7	14	27	57	200	22
7–10	6	7	9	13	22	42	87	282	33
6–10	9	11	13	20	32	57	125	354	46
5–10	12	15	18	27	48	84	169	438	62
4–10	14	19	24	37	64	112	215	504	78
3–10	16	22	30	45	83	143	267	570	95
2–10	17	25	34	54	101	184	332	634	114
1–10	21	31	44	70	133	240	408	714	142

Fig 3.3 Estimates of prevalence of disability among adults in Great Britain by age and severity category

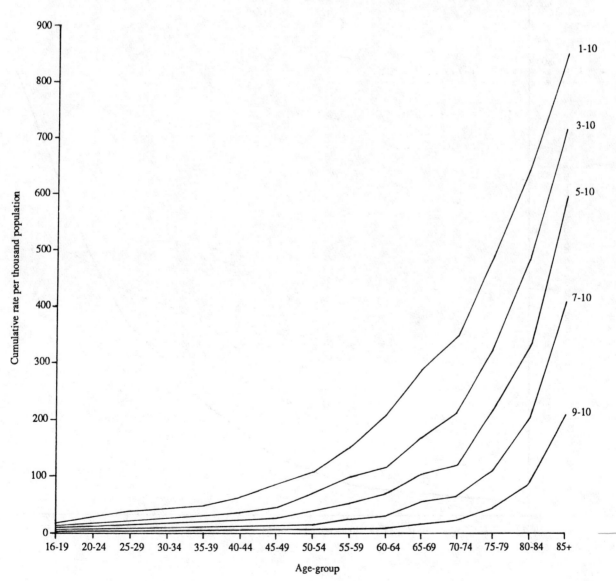

Figure 3.3 which illustrates the prevalence rates by five year age-groups for four selected bands of severity. This shows that the age above which prevalence rates start to rise steeply increases for successive severity bands. The prevalence of disability in categories 9 or 10 is quite low until people are in their late 60s after which there is a steep rise. The overall prevalence rates for all of severity categories 1 to 10 start to rise earlier and rise more gradually. The slope rises more steeply after about age 50 and even more so after age 70 so that from about age 75 more people have a disability at the level of severity included on the survey than do not.

As explained previously, the overall prevalence of disability depends on the concepts and methods used and so there is no reason why the estimates from this study should bear any direct relationship to those derived from other sources. However, comparisons can be useful in drawing attention to the relative nature of the estimates.

In Table 3.5 we show estimates from the 1985 General Household Survey (GHS) of limiting long-standing illness or disability compared with the disability survey estimates for all severity levels for the private household population, by five-year age-bands. The two sets of figures are illustrated in Figure 3.4. The GHS estimates are derived from answers to two questions:

'Do you have any long-standing illness, disability or infirmity? By long-standing I mean anything that has troubled you over a period of time or that is likely to affect you over a period of time.'

'Does this illness or disability limit your activities in any way?'

Those answering 'Yes' to both questions are included in the estimates shown in Table 3.5. Note that the second question is asked only if the first is answered positively.

Overall the GHS prevalence estimate for 1985 is higher than our survey estimate: 208 compared with 135 per

Fig 3.4 GHS estimates of prevalence of limiting longstanding disability by age (Great Britain 1985) compared with disability survey estimates: adults in private households

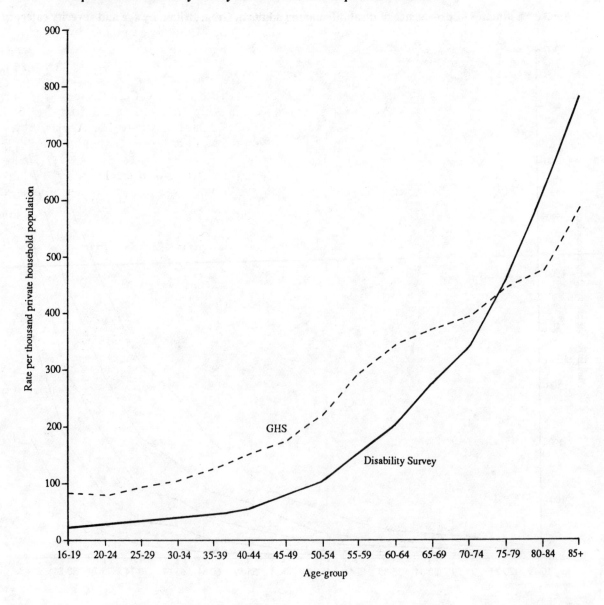

Table 3.5 GHS estimates of prevalence of limiting longstanding disability by age (Great Britain 1985) compared with disability survey estimates: rate per thousand private household population

Age group	GHS	Disability Survey
	Rate per thousand	
16–19	78	21
20–24	76	27
25–29	90	31
30–34	105	40
35–39	127	44
40–44	144	59
45–49	172	79
50–54	223	106
55–59	296	155
60–64	345	205
65–69	369	275
70–74	391	342
75–79	449	466
80–84	477	616
85 and over	588	779
16–59	139	58
60 and over	399	355
All 16 and over	208	135

lower estimates among the elderly.

Recently the Disability Alliance published a report claiming that there are three million disabled people in Great Britain. This estimate was based on results from the 1969 OPCS survey updated to take account of population changes and with additions for the groups of people not covered by that survey. The big difference between this estimate and that obtained by the present survey illustrates the effect that different definitions and methods can have on estimates. As we argued in Chapter 2, there is no *absolute* estimate of the number of disabled people in the country because of the continuous nature of the concept of disability; the level above which people are classified as disabled determines the number of people included.

3.4 Estimates of disability by severity and sex

Tables 3.6 and 3.7 show the estimates presented in Tables 3.3 and 3.4 separately for men and women, but for simplicity show only three age bands. Table 3.6 shows that there are considerably more disabled women than men at all except the lowest severity levels. In total there are around 3.6 million disabled women compared with just over 2.5 million disabled men in the country as a whole. The preponderance of women is apparent among both those in private households and those in communal establishments. However, women outnumber men substantially only at higher ages.

To discover whether this is due to the greater longevity of women the prevalence rates are compared in Table 3.7 and illustrated in Figure 3.5. Among those aged under 75 the prevalence of disability is roughly equal between men and women at all severity levels. But among those aged 75 or over, the rates for women are consistently higher than those for men. Among those

thousand. This was to be expected because any limitation in activities is counted for the GHS estimate whereas this survey asked questions about specific activities and only limitations in performing these activities were included in the definition of disability. What is surprising is the lower prevalence estimates for age 75 onwards obtained by the GHS compared with this survey; Figure 3.4 shows the lines cross and diverge above this age. We suggest that the reason for this is that many elderly people do not think of themselves as having health problems or being disabled; they consider limitations in activities a normal consequence of old age. On the GHS this probably means that some answer negatively to the first question and thus do not get asked the second, while others who answer 'Yes' to the first do not admit to any effect on their activities because they have come to accept their limitations. Both result in

Fig 3.5 Estimates of prevalence of disability among adults by age and severity category for men and women

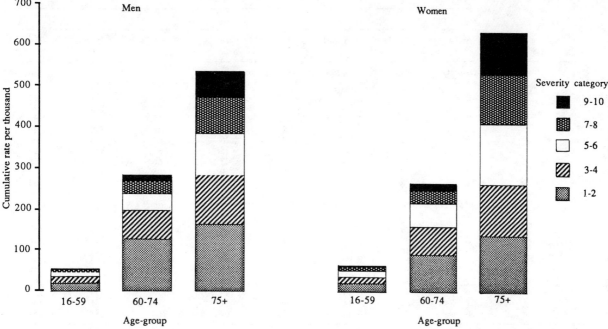

Table 3.6   Estimates of numbers of disabled adults in Great Britain by age and severity category for men and women (thousands)

Severity category	Men				Women			
	Age-group				Age-group			
	16–59	60–74	75 and over	Total	16–59	60–74	75 and over	Total
In private households (thousands)								
10	11	11	11	**33**	15	10	44	**69**
9	25	38	42	**105**	42	50	88	**180**
8	44	48	41	**133**	56	54	96	**205**
7	56	51	46	**152**	75	78	142	**295**
6	70	54	43	**167**	101	99	145	**345**
5	93	88	65	**246**	131	137	165	**433**
4	101	105	67	**273**	139	130	134	**403**
3	115	132	67	**314**	123	152	142	**417**
2	119	185	83	**387**	111	177	148	**437**
1	228	271	105	**605**	202	216	163	**581**
Total	861	983	570	**2,414**	994	1,101	1,269	**3,365**
In communal establishments (thousands)								
10	12	6	13	**31**	7	8	61	**77**
9	6	4	10	**20**	5	9	47	**60**
8	5	4	9	**18**	6	5	29	**40**
7	3	2	5	**11**	2	3	23	**27**
6	3	4	6	**12**	2	2	18	**22**
5	3	2	4	**9**	3	2	15	**20**
4	4	3	3	**10**	1	3	13	**17**
3	2	2	3	**6**	1	2	9	**12**
2	2	2	2	**6**	1	2	7	**10**
1	3	2	2	**7**	1	2	3	**6**
Total	43	31	57	**130**	29	38	225	**291**
Total population (thousands)								
10	23	17	24	**64**	22	18	105	**146**
9	31	42	52	**125**	47	59	135	**240**
8	49	52	50	**151**	62	59	125	**245**
7	59	53	51	**163**	77	81	165	**322**
6	73	58	49	**179**	103	101	163	**367**
5	96	90	69	**255**	134	139	180	**453**
4	105	108	70	**283**	140	133	147	**420**
3	117	134	70	**320**	124	154	151	**429**
2	121	187	85	**393**	112	179	155	**447**
1	231	273	107	**612**	203	218	166	**587**
Total	904	1,014	627	**2,544**	1,023	1,139	1,494	**3,656**

Table 3.7   Estimates of prevalence of disability among adults by age and severity category for men and women (cumulative rate per thousand population)

Severity category	Men				Women			
	Age-group				Age-group			
	16–59	60–74	75 and over	Total	16–59	60–74	75 and over	Total
In private households (cumulative rate per thousand)								
10	1	3	10	**2**	1	2	20	**3**
9–10	2	14	48	**7**	4	14	61	**11**
8–10	5	27	86	**13**	7	27	105	**20**
7–10	8	42	128	**21**	12	45	171	**34**
6–10	13	57	167	**29**	18	68	238	**49**
5–10	19	82	226	**41**	26	100	314	**68**
4–10	25	112	287	**54**	35	130	376	**86**
3–10	32	149	349	**69**	43	166	442	**105**
2–10	40	202	425	**88**	50	208	510	**125**
1–10	54	278	521	**117**	63	258	586	**151**
Total population including establishments (cumulative rate per thousand)								
10	1	5	21	**3**	1	4	45	**6**
9–10	3	17	64	**9**	4	18	102	**17**
8–10	6	31	107	**16**	8	31	154	**28**
7–10	10	46	150	**24**	13	50	224	**42**
6–10	14	62	191	**32**	19	73	293	**58**
5–10	20	87	250	**45**	28	106	369	**78**
4–10	27	117	309	**58**	36	136	431	**97**
3–10	34	155	369	**73**	44	172	495	**115**
2–10	41	207	442	**92**	51	213	561	**135**
1–10	56	283	533	**121**	64	264	631	**161**

Table 3.8 Estimates of numbers of disabled adults in Great Britain by region and severity category (thousands)

Severity category	North	Yorks and Humber-side	North West	East Mid-lands	West Mid-lands	East Anglia	GLC	South East	South West	Wales	Scotland	Great Britain
In private households (thousands)												
10	6	7	14	6	10	0	10	15	14	11	10	102
9	19	29	34	19	26	12	30	48	20	19	29	285
8	17	33	33	17	37	11	50	60	30	17	33	338
7	33	35	44	26	50	18	56	72	47	28	39	447
6	34	45	59	38	51	13	54	91	36	42	49	511
5	46	71	74	45	64	23	73	123	53	38	70	679
4	44	61	91	47	62	16	56	117	59	49	73	676
3	60	68	85	47	64	30	80	116	65	46	71	732
2	52	84	84	54	82	29	95	131	70	53	89	824
1	77	131	128	88	94	40	124	235	86	57	125	1,186
Total	389	566	644	387	541	194	628	1,007	480	359	587	5,780
In communal establishments (thousands)												
10	4	9	14	12	6	1	14	23	12	6	5	108
9	3	6	11	7	6	2	9	18	9	5	4	80
8	2	6	8	5	4	1	8	12	6	3	3	58
7	2	4	5	4	2	1	5	7	5	1	3	39
6	1	5	4	3	2	1	3	8	3	2	2	34
5	1	3	3	3	2	1	4	5	4	0	3	29
4	1	4	3	2	2	0	4	5	4	1	2	27
3	1	2	2	1	1	1	3	4	3	1	1	19
2	1	2	2	1	1	1	2	4	1	1	1	16
1	0	1	2	2	1	0	2	3	1	0	0	13
Total	16	42	55	40	27	9	54	89	47	20	24	422
Total population (thousands)												
10	10	16	28	18	16	1	24	38	26	17	15	210
9	22	35	45	26	32	14	39	66	29	24	33	365
8	19	39	41	22	41	12	58	72	36	20	36	396
7	35	39	49	30	52	19	61	79	52	29	42	486
6	35	50	63	41	53	14	57	99	39	44	51	545
5	47	74	77	48	66	24	77	128	57	38	73	708
4	45	65	94	49	64	16	60	122	62	50	75	704
3	61	70	87	48	65	31	83	120	68	47	72	750
2	53	86	86	55	83	30	97	135	71	54	90	840
1	77	132	130	90	95	40	126	238	87	57	125	1,198
Total	405	608	698	427	568	203	682	1,096	527	379	611	6,202

Table 3.9 Estimates of prevalence of disability among adults by region and severity category (cumulative rate per thousand population)

Severity category	North	Yorks and Humber-side	North West	East Mid-lands	West Mid-lands	East Anglia	GLC	South East	South West	Wales	Scotland	Great Britain
In private households (cumulative rate per thousand)												
10	2	2	3	2	3	0	2	2	4	5	2	2
9–10	10	9	10	8	9	8	7	8	9	14	10	9
8–10	17	18	16	14	18	15	17	15	18	22	18	17
7–10	31	27	25	23	31	27	27	24	31	34	28	27
6–10	45	39	37	35	43	36	37	35	41	53	40	39
5–10	64	58	52	50	59	51	51	50	56	71	58	55
4–10	83	74	70	65	75	61	61	65	73	93	76	71
3–10	108	92	88	81	91	81	76	79	91	114	94	88
2–10	130	114	105	99	112	100	94	95	110	138	116	107
1–10	162	148	130	128	135	127	117	124	135	164	147	135
1–10 stan-dardised for age	162	148	131	131	141	123	119	123	124	160	131	135
Total population (cumulative rate per thousand)												
10	4	4	6	6	4	1	4	5	7	8	4	5
9–10	13	13	15	14	12	10	11	13	15	19	12	13
8–10	21	23	23	21	22	18	22	21	25	27	21	22
7–10	35	33	32	31	35	30	33	31	39	41	31	33
6–10	50	46	45	44	48	39	44	43	50	60	44	46
5–10	69	65	60	60	64	55	58	58	65	77	61	62
4–10	87	82	79	76	80	65	69	73	83	100	80	78
3–10	112	100	96	91	96	85	84	87	101	121	98	95
2–10	134	122	113	109	116	104	102	104	121	145	120	114
1–10	166	156	139	138	139	130	125	132	145	170	151	142

aged 60–74, although the prevalence rates do not generally differ between men and women, the overall prevalence rate is higher for men than women, that is when those in severity category 1 have been included. More detailed analysis by five-year age-groups showed this difference is confined to the 60–64 year age band. The different retirement ages of men and women seems likely to be significant, but exactly what causes this difference is not clear. For some reason, men of this age seem more likely than women to report health problems or disabilities on the survey which are sufficient to include them in severity category 1 but not at higher levels.

The difference in numbers of men and women in the older age-groups occurs largely because women on average live longer than men. Differences in the rates per thousand of the population are more apparent for the total population than for the private household population reflecting the relatively large numbers of very elderly disabled women living in communal establishments. For example, more detailed analysis shows that, among those aged 85 and over, the overall rates of disability were 761 and 785 for men and women respectively among those living in private households, while the corresponding rates for the total population were 752 for men and 852 for women.

3.5 Estimates of disability by severity and region
Tables 3.8 and 3.9 give estimates of the numbers of disabled adults and prevalence rates for each of the standard regions of England and for Wales and Scotland. It is important to note that these are not the same as the National Health Service regional health authorities. The estimates for people living in institutions should be treated with some caution as there were some difficulties in applying regional boundaries to this sample. Clearly the numbers in each region can be expected to vary in line with the numbers in the population, so the prevalence rates are of greater interest. These show that Wales, the North, Yorkshire and Humberside and Scotland have the highest overall prevalence rates, while the lowest overall rates are found in the GLC area, the rest of the South East and East Anglia. However, the pattern is not always quite the same at all severity levels.

Differences between regions may be due to differences in the age structure of the population. Table 3.9 therefore also shows the effect of standardising the overall prevalence estimates for age. The standardised rates are those that a region would be expected to have if its age distribution were the same as that of Great Britain. For convenience the standardisation was carried out only on the private household figures; a similar picture would emerge if the total population figures had been used. Standardisation has a substantial effect only on the estimates for Scotland and the South West, both of which fell indicating that their populations are on average older than that of the country as a whole. Despite standardisation for age, regional differences are still apparent; thus either the populations in different regions differ in other respects related to disability or there are genuine regional differences in the prevalence of disability.

3.6 Estimates of disability by ethnic group
According to estimates from the Labour Force Survey (LFS), only 4% of the population of Great Britain belongs to an ethnic minority group. Therefore even on a survey of this size the number of people from an ethnic minority group identified on the survey is likely to be very small. Moreover, on a survey of disability the problem is exacerbated by the relationship between disability and age. Ethnic minority groups have far higher proportions of people in the younger age-groups than the white population and so, other things being equal, we would expect them to have a lower prevalence of disability. This means that in order to compare the prevalence rates for different ethnic groups it is essential to standardise for age. The only reliable source of population estimates by age for ethnic minority groups is the Labour Force Survey, which covers only the private household population. Table 3.10 shows the overall prevalence rates for the two largest ethnic minority groups, West Indians and Asians, compared with those for whites. The unstandardised rate for whites is far higher than that of either of the other groups, but after standardising for age the differences between the three groups are no longer significant.

Table 3.10   Estimates of prevalence of disability among adults in private households in Great Britain by ethnic group: standardised for age

Ethnic group	Unstandardised: rate per thousand	Standardised for age: rate per thousand
White	140	137
West Indian	57	151
Asian	74	126

3.7 Estimates by type of disability
In order to obtain an overall measure of severity of disability, we first developed scales of severity for a number of different areas of disability. Details of the development of the measures are given in Chapter 7. Thirteen areas of disability contributed to the overall measure and scales of severity were devised for eleven. In the remaining two areas there was insufficient information to develop scales of severity; there was merely sufficient to determine whether or not someone had a disability in these areas. The relatively large number of measures was required because of the way in which they were developed; we did not want any one area to have too wide a coverage for reasons explained in Chapter 7. The areas are:

Locomotion
Reaching and stretching
Dexterity
Seeing
Hearing
Personal care
Continence

Table 3.11 Estimates of numbers of disabled adults in Great Britain with different types of disability (thousands)

Type of disability	In private households	In establishments	Total population
	Thousands		
Locomotion	4,005	327	4,332
Reaching and stretching	1,083	147	1,230
Dexterity	1,572	165	1,737
Seeing	1,384	284	1,668
Hearing	2,365	223	2,588
Personal care	2,129	354	2,483
Continence	957	185	1,142
Communication	989	213	1,202
Behaviour	1,172	175	1,347
Intellectual functioning	1,182	293	1,475
Consciousness	188	41	229
Eating, drinking, digesting	210	66	276
Disfigurement	391	..	..

. . data not available

Fig 3.6   Estimates of prevalence of disability among adults in Great Britain by type of disability

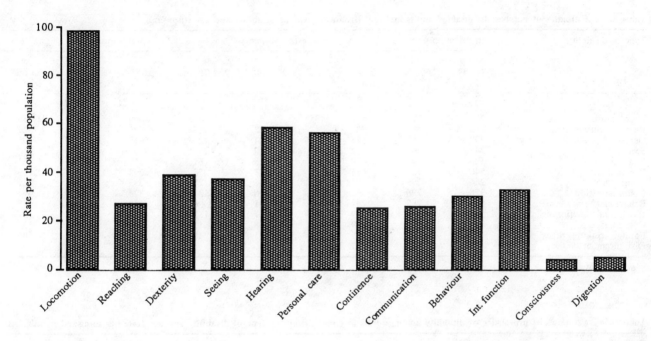

Communication
Behaviour
Intellectual functioning
Consciousness
Eating, drinking, digesting
Disfigurement

The last two are not strictly speaking disabilities, but covered a few relatively uncommon problems which did not result in disabilities covered by the other scales. Consciousness includes the types of disabilities resulting from having fits or convulsions.

Table 3.11 gives estimates derived from the surveys of the numbers of people in the population with disabilities in each of the above disability areas, while Table 3.12 shows the numbers from Table 3.11 expressed as rates per thousand of the population. These results are illustrated in Figure 3.6.

In the population as a whole, locomotor problems are the most common type of disability; over 4 million adults have this type of disability, a rate of 99 per

thousand of the population. Around two and a half million adults suffer from hearing and personal care disabilities respectively (59 and 57 per thousand respectively). The most common disabilities overall are experienced predominantly by those living in private households. As Chapter 4 will show, many of these disabilities were at the lower end of the severity range. Disabilities in areas such as intellectual functioning are proportionately more common among those living in communal establishments rather than in private households, partly because a higher proportion of people with such problems are at the higher end of the severity range.

Tables 3.13 and 3.14 are similar to the previous two tables but show the results separately for the under 60s, those aged 60–74 and those aged 75 or over. The most noticeable feature of the estimates of numbers is the huge differences between the most elderly group and the two younger groups in the establishment population for almost all types of disability. This is not apparent for most disabilities in the private household population, but may be due to different numbers in the population

25

Table 3.12 Estimates of prevalence of disability among adults in Great Britain by type of disability (rate per thousand population)

Type of disability	In private households	Total population (including establishments)
	Rate per thousand	
Locomotion	93	99
Reaching and stretching	25	28
Dexterity	37	40
Seeing	32	38
Hearing	55	59
Personal care	50	57
Continence	22	26
Communication	23	27
Behaviour	27	31
Intellectual functioning	28	34
Consciousness	4	5
Eating, drinking, digesting	5	6
Disfigurement	9	..

..data not available

in the different age-groups. The prevalence rates in Table 3.14 show increases with age for almost all types of disabilities, probably reflecting the importance of age-related complaints as a cause of disability. Although there is an increase with age, it is less acute for behavioural, intellectual functioning and consciousness disabilities compared with other types of disabilities.

Table 3.13 Estimates of numbers of disabled adults in Great Britain by type of disability and age (thousands)

Type of disability	In private households			In establishments			Total population		
	Age-group 16–59	60–74	75 and over	16–59	60–74	75 and over	16–59	60–74	75 and over
	Thousands								
Locomotion	974	1,520	1,511	35	45	247	1,009	1,565	1,758
Reaching and stretching	258	404	422	17	22	107	275	426	529
Dexterity	397	589	585	21	24	120	418	613	705
Seeing	247	405	732	46	40	198	293	445	930
Hearing	523	843	1,000	34	28	161	557	871	1,161
Personal care	546	728	856	47	53	253	593	781	1,109
Continence	266	299	393	27	31	128	293	330	521
Communication	328	296	365	48	36	129	376	332	494
Behaviour	604	280	287	46	31	98	650	311	385
Intellectual functioning	547	286	349	57	47	188	604	333	537
Consciousness	137	33	19	21	8	12	158	41	31
Eating, drinking, digesting	68	83	59	10	11	45	78	94	104
Disfigurement	163	141	87	..	..	..	..	..	..

..data not available

Table 3.14 Estimates of prevalence of disability among adults in Great Britain by type of disability and age (rate per thousand population)

Type of disability	In private households			Total (including establishments)		
	Age-group			Age-group		
	16–59	60–74	75 and over	16–59	60–74	75 and over
	Rate per thousand					
Locomotion	31	195	464	31	198	496
Reaching and stretching	8	52	129	9	54	149
Dexterity	12	76	180	13	78	199
Seeing	8	52	225	9	56	262
Hearing	16	108	307	17	110	328
Personal care	17	93	263	18	99	313
Continence	8	38	120	9	42	147
Communication	10	38	112	12	42	140
Behaviour	19	36	88	19	40	152
Intellectual functioning	17	37	107	20	40	109
Consciousness	4	4	6	5	10	9
Eating, drinking, digesting	2	11	18	2	12	30
Disfigurement	5	18	27	..	..	..

..data not available

4 Characteristics of disabled adults

4.1 Introduction

This chapter shows how the disabled adults interviewed on the surveys are distributed in terms of some of the main variables which will be used in later reports. The chapter is divided into two parts describing the private household and communal establishment samples respectively. All figures are expressed as percentages of the relevant group. For reasons explained more fully in Chapter 8, the total sample size has been set at 10,000 for the private household sample and 4,000 for the establishment sample. Weighting factors have been applied to correct for non-response and disproportionate sampling (interviewing only one in two of those aged 60 or over in the private household survey and taking a smaller proportion of large institutions in the establishment survey). The weighted bases roughly reflect the actual number of people interviewed. These results therefore give a good idea of the relative sizes of different subgroups available for more detailed analysis.

4.2 Adults living in private households

4.2.1 Age and sex distributions

Table 4.1 shows the age distribution for all disabled adults in private households both overall and for different severity bands. Adjacent severity categories have been combined to make the tables easier to read. The figures for three broad age bands are illustrated in Figure 4.1. Roughly a third of the total sample falls into each of the age bands under 60, 60 to 74 and 75 or over, but these proportions change with severity; the proportion in the two younger age bands decreases with

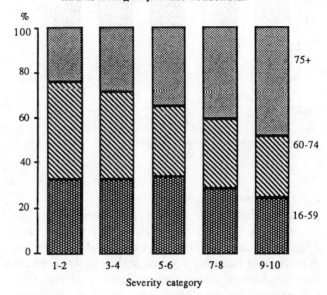

†Fig 4.1 Age distribution by severity category: adults living in private households

severity while the proportion in the oldest group rises. Thus only a quarter of those in severity categories 1 or 2 are 75 or over compared with almost half of those in categories 9 or 10.

Table 4.2 and Figures 4.2 and 4.3 show the age distributions for different severity bands separately for men and women. The preponderance of women over men at higher severity levels was noted in the previous chapter. Here we can see that not only are there higher proportions of disabled women than men aged 75 or over in total, but this is true at each level of severity. Moreover, the increase in the proportion aged 75 and over with severity noted on the previous table is much steeper for women than for men.

Table 4.1 Age distribution by severity category: adults living in private households

Age-group	Severity category					
	1–2	3–4	5–6	7–8	9–10	Total
	%	%	%	%	%	%
16–19	1	1	2	1	3	1
20–24	2	2	3	2	2	2
25–29	2	2	3	2	2	2
30–34	2	3	3	3	2	3
35–39	3	3	3	3	2	3
40–44	3	4	4	3	2	3
45–49	5	4	4	4	3	4
50–54	6	5	5	4	4	5
55–59	9	9	7	7	5	8
60–64	13	12	9	8	7	11
65–69	14	12	10	10	11	12
70–74	16	14	12	12	9	14
75–79	13	14	15	15	14	14
80–84	9	10	11	14	15	11
85 and over	3	5	9	13	19	7
16–59	33	33	34	29	25	31
60–74	43	38	31	30	27	37
75 and over	25	29	35	42	48	32
Total	100	100	100	100	100	100
Base:	*3,475*	*2,436*	*2,059*	*1,359*	*669*	*10,000*

Table 4.2 Age distribution by severity category for men and women: adults living in private households

	Severity category					
	1–2	3–4	5–6	7–8	9–10	Total
Men	%	%	%	%	%	%
16–59	35	37	40	36	27	36
60–74	46	40	34	34	37	41
75 and over	19	23	25	30	36	23
Total	100	100	100	100	100	100
Base:	*1,715*	*1,019*	*702*	*476*	*231*	*4,142*
Women	%	%	%	%	%	%
16–59	31	32	30	26	23	29
60–74	39	34	30	26	24	33
75 and over	31	34	40	48	53	38
Total	100	100	100	100	100	100
Base:	*1,748*	*1,433*	*1,354*	*882*	*439*	*5,856*

Fig 4.2   Age distribution by severity category: men living in private households

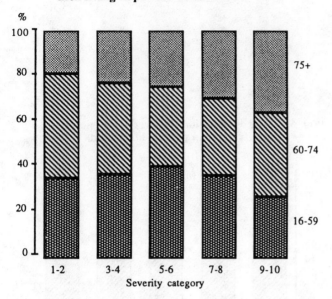

Fig 4.3   Age distribution by severity category: women living in private households

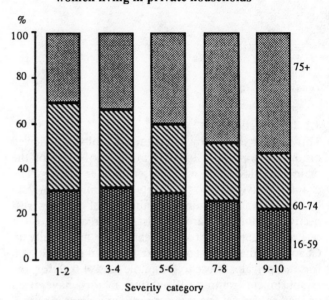

4.2.2 Complaints causing disability

At the beginning of the interview respondents were asked about the complaints giving rise to their disabilities. A diagnostic term was obtained if possible, but many people had only a vague notion of what caused their disabilities. There were particular problems with this question for the elderly, many of whom attributed their disabilities to old age rather than to any specific medical condition. This means that the information collected does not give a very accurate picture of the medical conditions causing disability. Nevertheless, we developed a classification based on a modification of the International Classification of Diseases (ICD) and coded the complaints mentioned accordingly. It should be noted that only complaints mentioned as a cause of a particular disability were included, and that people could have more than one complaint, even if they had only one disability. The classification has 16 main categories which correspond approximately to the ICD chapter headings. Most of the main categories are subdivided to show the common complaints causing disability.

Table 4.3 shows what proportion of the sample of disabled adults in private households mentioned each complaint as a cause of their disabilities. The numbers illustrate the problems in collecting and coding this kind of information. In many categories the proportion of complaints in the 'not elsewhere specified (nes)' or 'other' codes is much greater than in any of the specific codes. It is important to remember that these figures reflect the prevalence not the incidence of different complaints. Incidence is the number of new cases occurring during a given time period while prevalence is the number of cases at a given point in time and is consequently affected by the life expectancy associated with the different complaints. Thus a complaint with a high incidence and a short life expectancy may have a lower prevalence than one with a lower incidence but a longer life expectancy.

There is also a poor correspondence between the causes of death and the causes of disability. In the case of complaints causing disability, it is not only life expectancy, but life free from disability that is of relevance. A complaint which in its early stages does not affect daily activities will not feature in our survey as a cause of disability. A good example of this is some of the more common cancers. In their early stages they are not disabling and can often be cured. If they are fatal the time between the onset of disability and death is often quite short and so they do not feature as important causes of disability. In contrast complaints in the musculo-skeletal group such as arthritis have a slow onset with gradual deterioration in the ability to carry out daily activities but are not usually fatal and so feature as important causes of disability.

Table 4.3 shows that musculo-skeletal complaints were most frequently mentioned as the cause of disability, followed by ear complaints. Within the former category arthritis was most common, but most people did not know what sort of arthritis they had. Hardly any of those with ear complaints were able to specify the cause and generally just mentioned deafness or poor hearing. Likewise the category 'eye complaints' consisted mainly of people complaining of poor eyesight without specifying a cause.

Table 4.4 shows how the distribution of complaints cited as causes of disability varies according to severity category. Musculo-skeletal problems were the most common cause of disability at all severity levels except categories 1 to 2 where ear complaints were most common. Among the most severely disabled, those in categories 9 and 10, musculo-skeletal, nervous system, ear and eye complaints were the most common causes of disability, all of which include complaints with strong relationships with age.

Table 4.4 shows that some groups of complaints increase much more sharply with severity than others.

Table 4.3 Frequencies of complaints causing disability: adults living in private households

Classification of complaints	%
Infectious and parasitic	**1**
Neoplasms	**2**
Endocrine and metabolic	**2**
Diabetes	2
Osteomalacia/rickets	0
Obesity	0
Other endocrine and metabolic	1
Blood and blood-forming organs	**1**
Mental	**13**
Senile dementia	2
Schizophrenia	0
Anxiety and phobias	2
Depression	5
Other mental illness	3
Mental retardation	2
Nervous system	**13**
Stroke, hemiplegia	5
Parkinsons	1
Multiple sclerosis	1
Cerebral palsy	0
Paraplegia, quadraplegia etc.	0
Head injury	0
Epilepsy	2
Migraine	1
Other	3
Eye complaints	**22**
Cataract	5
Glaucoma	1
Congenital blindness	0
Caused by diabetes	0
Other	16
Ear complaints	**38**
Sensorineural deafness	1
Conductive deafness	2
Noise-induced deafness	2
Tinnitus	2
Deafness nes*	32
Other ear complaints	2
Circulatory system	**20**
Coronary artery disease	8
Valve disease	1
Hypertension	3
Other heart problems	4
Other arterial and embolic disease	4
Varicose veins, phlebitis, other circulatory	2

Classification of complaints	%
Respiratory system	**13**
Bronchitis and emphysema	6
Asthma and allergy	3
Industrial diseases	0
Sinusitis	0
Other	4
Digestive system	**6**
Stomach	1
Ulcer, dyspepsia, hiatus hernia	2
Hernia nes*	1
Other upper gastrointestinal tract	1
Other lower gastrointestinal tract	1
Genito-urinary system	**3**
Kidney disease	1
Other excretory problems	2
Reproductive system disorders	1
Skin disease or disorders	**1**
Musculo-skeletal system	**46**
Rheumatoid arthritis	4
Osteo-arthritis	7
Arthritis nes	20
Rheumatism	2
Back problems	6
Knee problems	1
Deformities	0
Absence or loss of extremity	1
Damage/delayed healing	5
Other	6
Congenital	**0**
Other and vague	**6**
Dizziness, vertigo	2
Dyslexia	0
Speech problems	0
Other complaints	0
Old age nes*	4

Percentages in a category do not add to totals as some people have more than one complaint
* Not elsewhere specified

Base = 10,000

Table 4.4 Frequency of complaints in ICD groups causing disability by severity category: adults living in private households

ICD groups	Severity category					Total
	1–2	3–4	5–6	7–8	9–10	
	% of disabled with complaints in each group					
Infections	1	1	1	1	1	1
Neoplasms	1	1	2	2	6	2
Endocrine	1	2	3	4	5	2
Blood	0	1	1	0	1	1
Mental	7	14	17	17	22	13
Nervous system	4	9	16	24	38	13
Eye	19	19	25	28	33	22
Ear	41	36	36	39	33	38
Circulatory	18	21	21	20	15	20
Respiratory	12	14	14	14	10	13
Digestive	4	5	7	8	5	6
Genito-urinary	1	3	4	5	7	3
Skin	1	1	1	1	2	1
Musculo-skeletal	36	46	54	58	44	46
Congenital	0	1	1	0	0	0
Other/vague	4	6	8	9	11	6
Base:	3,475	2,436	2,059	1,359	669	10,000

Percentages do not add to 100 as some people have more than one complaint

Fig 4.4 Frequency of each type of disability by severity: adults living in private households

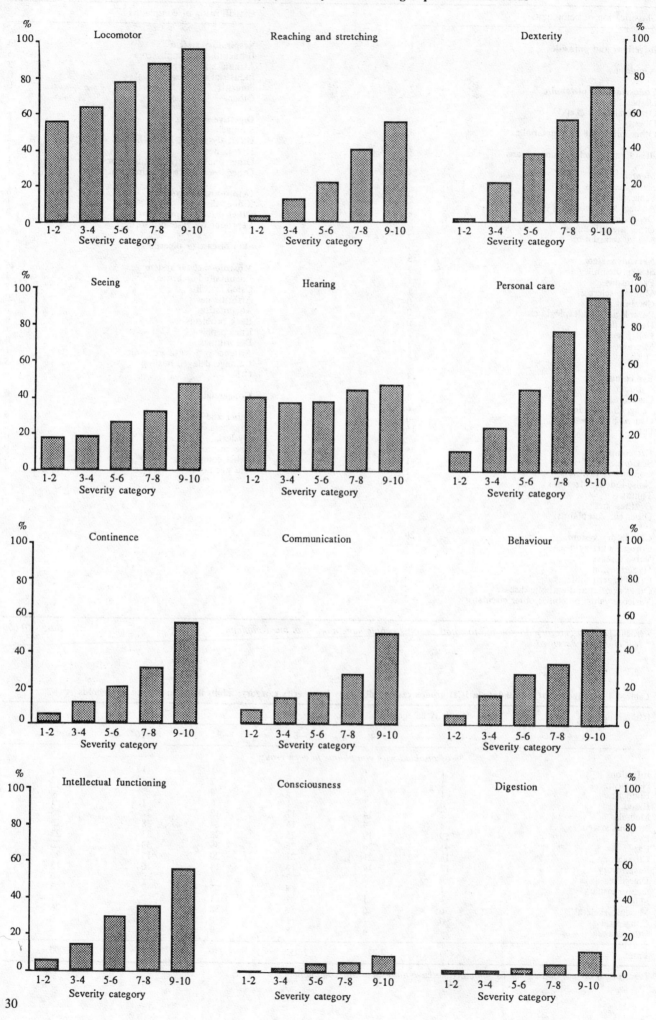

Complaints of the nervous system were mentioned as causes of disability by 4% of people in severity categories 1 to 2, but by 38% of those in categories 9 to 10. Mental complaints rise similarly from 7% to 22%. In contrast, the proportion of people citing ear, circulatory, respiratory and musculo-skeletal complaints as causes of disability does not increase consistently with severity. However, particularly among the more severely disabled, several complaints were often mentioned as causes of several disabilities, so not all the complaints listed by people in severity categories 9 and 10 necessarily result in disabilities at this level of severity; some may be ancillary to the main cause.

4.2.3 Different types of disability
Table 4.5 shows the proportion of disabled adults in private households with each of the thirteen types of disability. Over two thirds of the sample have a locomotor disability and 41% have a hearing disability. These figures of course reflect the preponderance of musculo-skeletal and ear complaints noted above. Personal care disabilities, while treated in the ICIDH as disabilities in their own right, can also be viewed as consequences of some of the other disabilities.

A similar problem to that described in the previous section affects the interpretation of Table 4.5 With increasing severity multiple disabilities become more common and so all types of disabilities are more common at higher than at lower severity levels, even if they are not always one of the three most severe disabilities which determine the severity category. The relative frequency of the different disabilities and the rate of increase with severity can be seen more clearly in Figure 4.4. Locomotor disabilities are most common, but do not increase very sharply with severity, whereas reaching, dexterity and personal care disabilities show steep rises with increasing severity.

Table 4.6 shows these results separately for the three age bands under 60, 60 to 74 and 75 and over. The prevalence of most disabilities increases with age, although for some the distinction is between the over 75s and the rest, rather than a consistent rise. Multiple disabilities are more common among the elderly than among younger disabled people. Communication, behavioural and intellectual functioning disabilities are more common among those aged under 60 than among the older disabled. This is because conditions such as mental handicap do not increase with age and are a major cause of disability at younger ages.

4.3 Adults living in communal establishments
4.3.2 Age and sex distributions
Table 4.7 shows the age distribution according to severity band for adults living in communal establishments. The main results are illustrated in Figure 4.5. This shows that the vast majority of disabled residents are elderly; two thirds are aged 75 or over and indeed just over half are aged 80 or over. Even at the lowest severity level, categories 1 and 2, half the residents were aged 75 or over and less than a quarter were under 60.

Table 4.8 and Figures 4.6 and 4.7 compare the age distributions in different severity bands separately for men and women. A much higher proportion of the women than the men were aged 75 or over (77% compared with 44%). This pattern is apparent at all severity levels. Although the results show that higher proportions of men than women are in the younger age-groups it is not the case that in absolute terms there are more younger disabled men than women. It is the higher mortality rates of men compared with women which results in fewer elderly disabled men than women and therefore correspondingly higher proportions at younger ages.

4.3.2 Complaints causing disability
Information was collected on each resident's long term health problems or complaints which gave rise to their disabilities. For this survey all complaints mentioned were assumed to cause disability, whereas on the private household survey questions were asked to establish whether this was in fact the case. The same classification was used as for the private household survey, with minor modifications at the detailed level to reflect the kinds of complaints which were common in this population. As with the private household survey individuals could and frequently did have more than one complaint

Table 4.5 Frequency of different types of disability by severity category: adults living in private households

Type of disability	Severity category					
	1–2	3–4	5–6	7–8	9–10	Total
	% of disabled with each disability					
Locomotion	56	64	78	88	96	69
Reaching and stretching	4	13	23	41	56	19
Dexterity	2	23	39	58	76	27
Seeing	18	19	27	33	48	24
Hearing	41	38	39	45	48	41
Personal care	12	25	46	78	97	37
Continence	5	12	20	31	56	17
Communication	8	15	18	28	51	17
Behaviour	6	17	29	35	54	20
Intellectual functioning	6	15	30	36	56	21
Consciousness	1	2	5	6	10	3
Eating, drinking, digesting	2	2	4	6	13	4
Disfigurement	4	6	7	11	16	7
Base:	*3,475*	*2,436*	*2,059*	*1,359*	*669*	*10,000*

Percentages do not add to 100 as some people have more than one type of disability

Table 4.6 Frequency of different types of disability by severity category and age: adults living in private households

Type of disability	Severity category					Total
	1–2	3–4	5–6	7–8	9–10	
Age 16 to 59: % with each disability						
Locomotion	44	44	58	73	90	53
Reaching and stretching	4	11	16	33	51	14
Dexterity	2	21	27	48	72	22
Seeing	13	8	13	19	31	13
Hearing	34	26	23	30	21	28
Personal care	12	19	36	64	93	30
Continence	5	12	16	30	50	14
Communication	9	15	21	30	51	18
Behaviour	11	32	48	56	62	33
Intellectual functioning	12	25	44	53	62	30
Consciousness	2	5	11	16	23	7
Eating, drinking, digesting	3	2	4	6	7	3
Disfigurement	7	8	9	13	19	9
Base:	*1,130*	*830*	*689*	*398*	*161*	*3,208*
Age 60 to 74: % with each disability						
Locomotion	62	70	84	93	96	73
Reaching and stretching	4	15	28	51	66	20
Dexterity	2	31	48	66	83	29
Seeing	15	17	24	30	34	20
Hearing	42	38	39	44	40	41
Personal care	12	27	47	84	98	35
Continence	5	12	21	30	45	14
Communication	7	14	14	26	46	14
Behaviour	3	12	21	26	44	13
Intellectual functioning	3	11	22	28	45	13
Consciousness	–	1	3	3	9	2
Eating, drinking, digesting	2	4	3	6	15	4
Disfigurement	4	7	8	12	20	7
Base:	*1,470*	*903*	*652*	*393*	*191*	*3,609*
Age 75 and over: % with each disability						
Locomotion	63	78	92	95	97	82
Reaching and stretching	5	13	27	45	52	24
Dexterity	2	16	43	65	75	33
Seeing	28	35	43	46	64	40
Hearing	50	52	55	59	64	55
Personal care	14	28	54	79	98	46
Continence	5	13	22	30	59	21
Communication	7	16	18	28	52	20
Behaviour	2	5	17	25	54	15
Intellectual functioning	4	9	23	29	55	19
Consciousness	–	–	2	2	3	1
Eating, drinking, digesting	1	1	4	4	10	3
Disfigurement	2	2	4	8	12	4
Base:	*864*	*719*	*715*	*566*	*317*	*3,181*

Table 4.7 Age distribution by severity category: adults living in communal establishments

Age-group	Severity category					Total
	1–2	3–4	5–6	7–8	9–10	
	%	%	%	%	%	%
16–19	1	0	0	0	0	0
20–24	2	0	1	1	3	2
25–29	3	1	3	2	3	3
30–34	1	2	2	3	2	2
35–39	3	2	3	2	2	2
40–44	4	3	3	2	2	2
45–49	2	3	1	2	1	2
50–54	2	3	2	1	2	2
55–59	5	3	4	2	2	3
60–64	5	3	3	3	4	3
65–69	10	8	3	5	4	5
70–74	13	10	9	6	7	8
75–79	16	18	14	16	15	15
80–84	22	20	23	20	19	20
85 and over	12	22	30	34	36	32
16–59	23	17	19	15	17	18
60–74	28	21	15	14	15	16
75 and over	50	60	67	70	70	67
Total	100	100	100	100	100	100
Base:	*272*	*436*	*598*	*912*	*1,782*	*4,000*

Fig 4.5 Age distribution by severity category: adults living in establishments

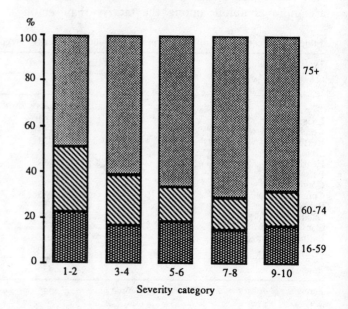

Table 4.8 Age distribution by severity category for men and women: adults living in communal establishments

| | Severity category | | | | | |
	1–2	3–4	5–6	7–8	9–10	Total
Men	%	%	%	%	%	%
16–59	34	32	29	29	36	32
60–74	34	31	25	20	21	24
75 and over	32	37	46	50	44	44
Total	100	100	100	100	100	100
Base:	*118*	*157*	*200*	*275*	*482*	*1,231*
Women	%	%	%	%	%	%
16–59	14	9	13	11	9	10
60–74	23	17	10	11	13	13
75 and over	63	74	77	78	79	77
Total	100	100	100	100	100	100
Base:	*154*	*279*	*398*	*638*	*1,300*	*2,769*

and so can be counted in more than one category. Table 4.9 shows the proportion of residents with each complaint both at the level of the 16 summary categories and for the more detailed classification.

The most common complaints by far, affecting a half of the sample, were some kind of mental dysfunction, notably senile dementia, mental handicap and psychoses. About a third of the residents had a musculo-skeletal disorder; 21% had some form of arthritis. This may be an under-estimate since some 'back problems', 'knee problems' and 'other skeletal' disorders are likely also to have arisen from arthritis. The third largest group of complaints was dysfunction of the nervous system, mainly strokes, epilepsy, and Parkinson's

disease. Complaints which were less prevalent but still made a noticeable contribution to disability were eye and ear complaints and disorders of the circulatory, digestive and genito-urinary systems.

Table 4.10 shows how the distributions of complaints according to the 16-category classification vary according to severity. Only complaints of the nervous system show a sharp increase with increasing severity.

4.3.3 Different types of disability
Table 4.11 and Figure 4.8 show how the distributions of different types of disability vary according to different severity bands. All types of disability are more common at higher severity levels because, as noted above, multiple disabilities are more common with increasing severity and indeed those in the higher severity categories must necessarily have more than one disability.

Table 4.12 shows how the results from the previous table vary with age. In general the frequency of disabilities which are likely to have physical causes increases with age (locomotor, reaching and stretching, and dexterity disabilities). The disabilities most likely to be associated with mental impairment or mental illness (intellectual functioning, behaviour, communication and consciousness disabilities) showed a decrease with age. This might be due either to people leaving institutions and moving back into the community or to the relatively high mortality rates associated with some of the conditions that cause these kinds of disabilities. Seeing, hearing and continence disabilities do not show consistent variation with age.

Fig 4.6 Age distribution by severity category: men living in establishments

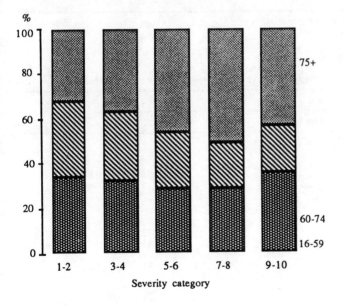

Fig 4.7 Age distribution by severity category: women living in establishments

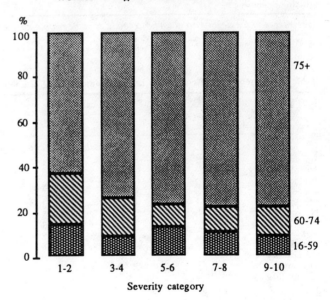

33

Table 4.9 Frequencies of complaints causing disability: adults living in communal establishments

Classification of complaints	%	Classification of complaints	%
Infectious and parasitic	0	**Circulatory system**	16
		Coronary artery disease	3
Neoplasms	4	Valve disease	0
Cancers	4	Hypertension	2
Benign growths	0	Other heart problems	6
		Other arterial and embolic disease	4
Endocrine and metabolic	8	Varicose veins, phlebitis, other circulatory	2
Diabetes	5		
Osteomalacia/rickets	0	**Respiratory system**	6
Obesity	1	Bronchits and emphysema	3
Other endocrine and metabolic	2	Asthma and allergy	1
		Industrial diseases	0
Blood and blood forming organs	2	Sinusitis	0
		Other	3
Mental	56		
Senile dementia	26	**Digestive system**	10
Schizophrenia	7	Stomach	0
Anxiety and phobias	2	Ulcers	4
Depression	6	Hernias	1
Other mental illness	4	Other upper gastronintestinal tract	2
Mental handicap	9	Other lower gastronintestinal tract	5
Severe mental handicap	6		
Other neuroses	1	**Genito-urinary system**	10
Other psychoses	5	Kidney disease	1
		Other excretory problems	9
Nervous system	30	Reproductive system disorders	1
Stroke, hemiplegia	14		
Parkinsons	4	**Skin disease or disorders**	2
Multiple sclerosis	1		
Cerebral palsy	2	**Musculo-skeletal system**	37
Paraplegia, quadraplegia etc.	1	Rheumatoid arthritis	2
Head injury	0	Osteo-arthritis	5
Epilepsy	7	Arthritis nes	14
Migraine	0	Rheumatism	1
Other CNS disease	3	Back problems	2
Other PNS disease	2	Knee problems	0
		Deformities	2
Eye complaints	17	Absence or loss of extremity	1
Cataract	3	Damage/delayed healing	5
Glaucoma	1	Other	14
Congenital blindness	0		
Other	13	**Congenital**	0
Ear complaints	13	**Other and vague**	10
Sensorineural deafness	12	Dizziness, vertigo	2
Conductive deafness	0	Speech problems	5
Noise-induced deafness	0	Other complaints	2
Tinnitus	0	Old age nes	2
Other	1		

Percentages in a category do not add to totals as some people have more than one complaint

Base = 4,000

Table 4.10 Frequency of complaints in ICD groups causing disability by severity category: adults living in communal establishments

ICD group	Severity category					
	1–2	3–4	5–6	7–8	9–10	Total
	% of disabled with complaints in each group					
Infections	0	1	–	0	0	0
Neoplasms	2	3	4	3	4	4
Endocrine	4	5	9	7	9	8
Blood	1	2	3	3	2	2
Mental	62	52	50	52	60	56
Nervous system	11	18	20	27	40	30
Eye	10	13	16	19	40	17
Ear	10	12	14	16	18	13
Circulatory	11	18	21	17	12	16
Respiratory	7	9	9	6	13	6
Digestive	9	12	10	9	5	10
Genito-urinary	2	4	5	6	11	10
Skin	2	1	2	2	17	2
Musculo-skeletal	23	33	37	38	3	37
Congenital	–	0	0	0	39	0
Other/vague	3	5	8	9	0	10
					12	
Base	272	436	598	912	1,782	4,000

Percentages do not add to 100 as some people have more than one complaint

Fig 4.8 Frequency of each type of disability by severity: adults living in establishments

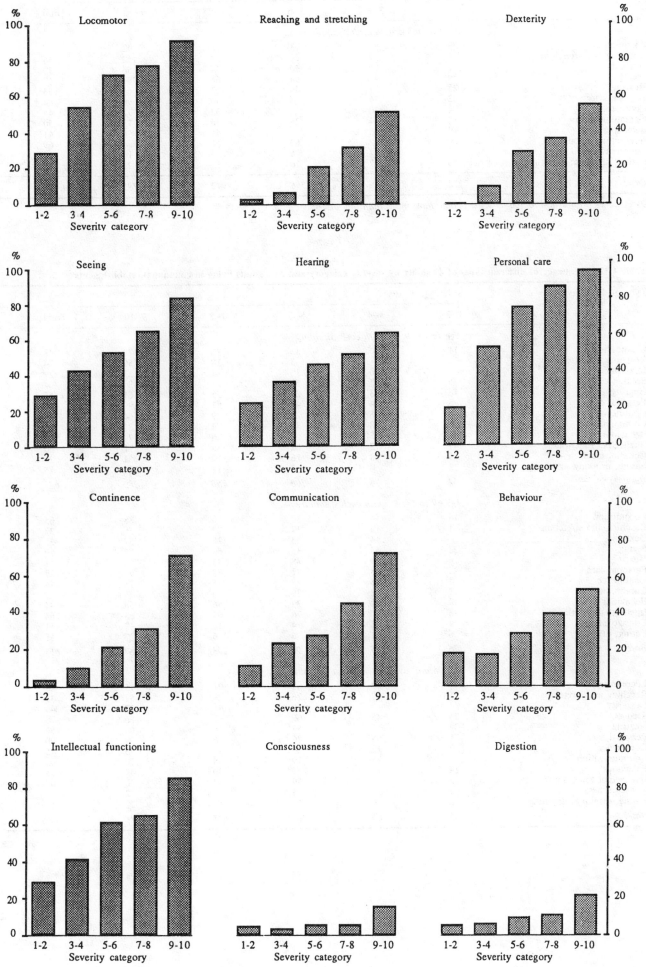

Table 4.11 Frequency of different types of disability by severity category: adults living in communal establishments

Type of disability	Severity category					Total
	1–2	3–4	5–6	7–8	9–10	
	% of disabled with each disability					
Locomotion	29	55	73	78	92	77
Reaching and stretching	3	7	21	32	52	35
Dexterity	1	10	30	37	56	39
Seeing	29	43	54	66	84	67
Hearing	25	37	46	52	64	53
Personal care	22	56	78	90	99	84
Continence	4	10	22	32	72	44
Communication	12	24	28	46	73	50
Behaviour	19	18	30	41	54	41
Intellectual functioning	29	42	62	66	86	69
Consciousness	5	4	6	6	16	10
Eating, drinking, digesting	6	7	10	12	23	15
Base:	272	436	598	912	1,782	4,000

Percentages do not add to 100 as some people have more than one disability

Table 4.12 Frequency of different types of disability by severity category and age: adults living in communal establishments

Type of disability	Severity category					Total
	1–2	3–4	5–6	7–8	9–10	
Age 16 to 59: % with each disability						
Locomotion	11	20	32	33	79	48
Reaching and stretching	–	–	5	10	50	24
Dexterity	–	10	16	14	53	29
Seeing	35	37	51	61	84	64
Hearing	18	33	27	55	61	47
Personal care	5	24	43	67	99	66
Continence	6	6	21	29	64	38
Communication	28	48	49	74	83	66
Behaviour	32	35	65	76	74	65
Intellectual functioning	49	73	64	88	91	80
Consciousness	5	13	16	17	51	29
Eating, drinking, digesting	3	4	7	11	25	15
Base:	62	76	108	150	282	679
Age 60 to 74: % with each disability						
Locomotion	16	44	58	66	88	65
Reaching and stretching	1	12	17	29	56	33
Dexterity	–	14	35	28	57	35
Seeing	32	43	35	63	78	59
Hearing	16	29	38	33	56	41
Personal care	22	48	81	87	98	77
Continence	4	8	33	35	78	44
Communication	15	32	39	50	76	52
Behaviour	19	22	33	56	58	44
Intellectual functioning	38	50	76	65	83	68
Consciousness	9	3	4	11	17	11
Eating, drinking, digesting	6	11	6	6	27	15
Base:	76	95	90	128	264	653
Age 75 and over: % with each disability						
Locomotion	44	69	88	91	95	88
Reaching and stretching	5	7	26	38	52	38
Dexterity	1	9	33	44	57	43
Seeing	25	45	60	67	86	70
Hearing	34	41	53	54	66	57
Personal care	31	68	86	96	99	90
Continence	3	12	20	32	73	45
Communication	4	15	19	38	70	46
Behaviour	14	12	20	30	49	35
Intellectual functioning	15	31	59	62	86	67
Consciousness	3	1	3	3	2	7
Eating, drinking, digesting	6	6	12	13	22	16
Base:	133	265	399	635	1,236	2,668

Part II Details of the survey methods

5 Design of the private household surveys

5.1 Introduction

The first major problem in carrying out a survey of disabled people living in private households lies in obtaining a sample of people to be interviewed. There is no comprehensive list of all disabled people in the country from which samples of disabled adults and children living in private households could be drawn. It was therefore necessary to screen a large sample of the general population in order to identify the adults and children with disabilities who were to be the subjects of the private household surveys.

This required a sample of the general population to be screened to identify those who were disabled, and a practical means of screening what would undoubtedly be a very large number of the population so as to identify as accurately as possible those who could be defined as disabled for the purposes of this study.

5.2 The sampling frame

An early decision was taken to use the Postcode Address File (PAF) as the source of the random sample of addresses to be screened to identify people with disabilities who would then be followed up and interviewed. The PAF is a list, compiled by the Post Office, of all addresses in the country to which mail is delivered. The 'small-user' part of the PAF lists all addresses which receive on average less than twenty items of mail per day. Its coverage of the private household population is known to be very good, but it does include a proportion of non-residential addresses, small institutions and addresses with more than one resident household, all groups requiring special treatment.[1] The great advantage of the PAF for sampling purposes is that it is computerised and kept up to date. This enabled the whole screening operation to be carried out more quickly and cheaply than would have been possible with any other frame.

5.3 Choice of screening method

The next decision was whether to use a postal or personal approach to screen addresses to identify people with disabilities. A number of factors affected the choice.

A major factor was the relative cost. Considering the screening phase on its own, it would clearly be cheaper to use a postal approach. However, if the screening phase were integrated with the interviews with disabled people, the cost advantage of postal screening would be less apparent, particularly in urban areas.

The cost considerations had to be weighed against expected levels of response with the two methods. Although OPCS has in the past obtained high levels of response to postal questionnaires, a personal approach was still expected to produce higher response rates than a postal approach. A high response rate minimises the risk of non-response bias. We were particularly concerned about the possibility of non-response bias with respect to disability at the screening phase. On the one hand, households not containing a disabled person would be asked questions about health problems and disabilities that they did not have, and the lack of relevance to them might make them less likely to respond. On the other hand, people with disabilities, particularly the elderly living alone, might find it difficult to fill in the screening questionnaire and therefore be less likely to respond.

A further problem which applies particularly in urban areas is that, as noted earlier, the PAF does not always accurately identify addresses containing more than one household. If one screening questionnaire is sent to an address it is difficult to ensure that it has been seen and completed by all the people living at the address if they are in different households.

A considerable amount of preliminary work was devoted to developing and testing the screening procedures, and a major feasibility study was carried out to compare the two methods and to provide sufficient information to determine the number of addresses which would need to be screened in the main survey in order to achieve full interviews with at least 10,000 disabled adults and to provide cost estimates for the main survey.

Several versions of the screening questionnaire were tested before the main feasibility study; interviewers checked people's answers with them to ensure that, as far as possible, the questions were understood and the instructions followed correctly. For the feasibility study three separate samples of 1,500 addresses were screened initially: two samples of 1,500 addresses in the same 25 areas were screened by post and by interviewers respectively. This allowed postal and interviewer screening methods to be compared. A further unclustered sample of 1,500 addresses was screened by post to give a better estimate of the yield of the screening questionnaire than could be obtained from the clustered samples. Addresses screened by post in the 25 areas where interviewers were working were followed up by an interviewer if they failed to reply after two reminders. Checks were also made by interviewers on the intelligibility of the questions and the accuracy of the answers to the screening questions. A special check was made by interviewers on addresses containing anyone aged 80 or over who had not mentioned any disability.

Analysis of the results of this study showed:

(a) A satisfactory level of response to a postal approach could be obtained in most areas (84% of forms were returned), but a significantly lower response rate was obtained in inner city areas.

(b) Analysis of the characteristics of respondents screened by post and by interviewers, and of non-responders to the postal approach who were contacted by interviewers, did not provide any evidence of serious non-response bias with respect to disability once differences in the age distributions had been taken into account. However, the numbers on which this analysis were based were small and so the results were treated with some caution.

(c) Interviewer checks on information provided by post indicated a high level of accuracy. Where there were problems it seemed that people were being screened in who should have been excluded rather than that disabled people were being missed. In particular, people with health problems which did not cause any disability seemed anxious to tell us about them, although it was not intended to screen in such people. The check on people aged 80 or over who had not reported a disability did not indicate that they in fact had disabilities which were being missed.

(d) Multi-household addresses were not accurately identified from returned postal questionnaires and the correct people had not always been screened. The majority of such addresses were in inner city areas.

On this study a high proportion of people were screened in as disabled, partly because some of the questions were rather vague, but also because people with minor impairments but little or no disability were answering positively to the screening questionnaire, mainly in response to a general 'anything else?' question at the end. Revision of the screening questionnaire meant that the estimates of the yield were no longer valid and so a further trial based on 1,000 addresses was required to obtain a revised estimate.

5.4 The initial screening phase
5.4.1 The sift sample design and procedures
On the basis of the feasibility work it was estimated that a sample of 100,000 addresses would be required to achieve interviews with 10,000 disabled adults and around 2,000 disabled children using the particular set of screening questions which had been developed. The sample of addresses was selected from the PAF. The PAF divides Great Britain into about 8,500 postal sectors which the OPCS frame further combines into some 8,000 areas each containing a minimum of 500 addresses. The first stage was to sample 500 of these

areas with probability proportional to size. The sectors were stratified by region, by a metropolitan/non-metropolitan split and finally within these divisions were systematically ordered by the proportion of people above retirement age. The second stage was to select 200 addresses from each of the selected areas, producing a total of 100,000 addresses.

In 400 of the areas (covering 80,000 addresses) the screening was carried out by post. A short questionnaire was sent to the occupier of the address, who was also asked to indicate if there were any other households living there. If this was so, that address was re-allocated to an interviewer for personal screening. In the remaining 100 areas interviewers delivered the screening questionnaire personally. These 100 areas included the whole of Inner London, the Clydeside conurbation and other inner city areas. Such areas contain the highest concentrations of multi-household addresses and response to postal questionnaires tends to be poor.

Occupiers of non-residential addresses, such as business premises, were asked to indicate that there were no permanent residents at the address. Residents were asked to answer questions about a variety of difficulties with everyday activities and some health problems in relation to each member of the household. In addition they were asked to give the age and sex of everyone living in the household permanently. This information was required to calculate national estimates as described in Chapter 8.

The success of the postal screening method used for the majority of addresses depends on an adequate response rate and an acceptable quality of replies to the questions. Despite extensive pilot work to ensure these criteria were met there was concern about the possibility of disability-related non-response bias. Interviewers can generally be expected to achieve higher levels of response than a postal approach. At the main screening stage, therefore, a sample of one in ten addresses which failed to return a questionnaire by post after two reminder letters were followed up by interviewers who attempted to obtain a completed screening questionnaire.

5.4.2 Response at the screening stage
The postal screening stage took place in March—May 1985. Of the 80,000 questionnaires sent out by post, 83% were returned after up to two reminder letters. However, this figure includes those returned by the Post Office or by other people because the address did not exist or was vacant, or where the reply indicated that there were no permanent residents at the address. Some of the non-responding addresses would also be of this type; the follow-up of a sample of non-responding addresses allowed us to estimate how many of these there were likely to be and thus to estimate the total number of addresses which contained permanent residents. On this basis the response from addresses thought to contain permanent residents was calculated to be 82%. This figure also excludes a small number of questionnaires which were returned with an explicit refusal to complete the form.

The interviewer screening stage began in July 1985. Since interviews with those identified as having disabilities were arranged immediately, the screening continued throughout the main fieldwork period, until October 1985. As expected, response to the screening carried out by interviewers was higher than for the postal approach. About 18% of the 20,000 addresses were found to be non-residential and some addresses were found to contain more than one household. The response rate among households with permanent residents was 86%. Table 5.1 gives details of the response at the initial screening stage.

The one-in-ten sample of addresses which did not return a postal questionnaire and which were followed up by an interviewer comprised about 1,500 addresses. Interviewers obtained the required screening information from 81%, providing a reasonable basis for investigating non-response bias. Comparison of disability rates estimated from the main postally screened samples and this sample of non-responding addresses did not reveal evidence of significant non-response bias with respect to disability and provided no justification for weighting the estimates. Details of this investigation are given in Chapter 8.

As mentioned above, the PAF sample of addresses included a number of small institutions which contained varying numbers of permanent residents. Since surveys of disabled people living in communal establishments were being carried out separately it was important to have a clear divide between the two kinds of surveys to ensure people were neither missed nor counted twice. It was decided to exclude from the private household survey sample any institution with four or more permanent residents that was specifically for the elderly, the disabled, or for children. All institutions were asked to state the number of permanent residents on the screening questionnaire and all with the exception of those listed above were visited by an interviewer to obtain screening information for each resident.

5.4.3 Preliminary identification of people with disabilities

The screening questionnaire contained questions about difficulties with everyday activities and some health problems, and was completed with respect to both adults and children in a household. The form-filler was asked to give the name, sex, date of birth and nature of the complaint or health problem of anyone who had one of the difficulties or health problems mentioned. This information allowed us to distinguish children from adults and to divide adults into those under 60 and those aged 60 or over, since only half of the latter group were to be interviewed. The sub-sampling of people aged 60 or over was done systematically from a list ordered by household within area and so ensured that only one person was selected from a household containing two elderly disabled people.

Positive answers to questions at the initial screening phase were not taken to mean that someone was necessarily disabled, but that there was sufficient indication of a problem to justify an interview which could collect more detailed information. It is more difficult to carry out screening accurately by means of a postal questionnaire than with an interviewer available to answer queries and check answers. Any postal questionnaires where the answers were unclear or ambiguous were treated as positive responses and included at the second stage so that an interviewer could check whether they should in fact be included. This meant that the proportion of addresses which appeared to contain at least one disabled person was higher among those screened by post than among those screened personally. This resulted in a higher proportion of the latter falling below the level set for being considered as disabled at the next stage, as described below.

5.5 Screening at the interview stage
Because of the problems of identifying accurately at the initial screening stage those people with disabilities of

Table 5.1 Response at the initial screening stage

	Method of screening:						
	Postal		Interviewer		Total		
	No.	%	No.	%	No.	%	
Addresses to screen	**80,000**	**100**	**20,000**	**100**	**100,000**	**100**	
Non-residential	2,727	3	2,869	15	5,596	6	
Post Office returns/does not exist	2,351	3	587	3	2,938	3	
Addresses with households	74,922	94	16,544	82	91,466	91	
Extra households			920		920		
Households to screen	**74,922**	**100**	**17,464**	**100**	**92,386**	**100**	
Sift form completed	59,982	80	15,094	86	75,076	81	
No one disabled	38,952	52	10,294	59	49,248	53	
Someone disabled	21,032	28	4,800	27	25,828	28	
Refusal/incomplete form	875	1	1,219	7	2,094	2	
Form not returned/non-contact	14,065	19	1,151	7	15,216	17	
Number of adults identified	**149,790**	**100**	**35,898**	**100**	**185,688**	**100**	
Number of adults screened in	23,277	16	5,138	14	28,415	15	

interest on the survey, the screening questionnaires were somewhat over-inclusive, particularly with respect to those disabilities that are most difficult to identify; notably those caused by mental or psychological problems. To compensate for this the first part of the main interview acted as a second screening stage. Answers given at the initial screening stage were checked and further questions were asked about some disabilities. On the basis of their answers some people were not considered to have a sufficiently severe level of disability to be included on the survey and the interview was terminated.

Originally the surveys aimed to achieve full interviews with about 10,000 disabled adults and 2,000 disabled children. The screening stages were designed to identify considerably more disabled adults than this. Allowance needed to be made for reductions in the numbers for several reasons: the selection of only half of those aged 60 or over for interview; the gap of several months between the postal screening and the main interviews, during which some people had died or entered an institution; and some non-response at the interview stage. Together these were estimated to bring the numbers down to approximately those necessary to achieve the numbers of full interviews mentioned above.

5.6 The main interview with disabled adults
Of those adults identified from the screening questionnaires as having some disability, some 18,000 were approached for interview. Whenever possible the disabled adult was interviewed personally, but if this was not possible a proxy interview was conducted with someone who was able to answer on their behalf. In most cases such interviews took place because the dis-

abled person was too ill or disabled to be interviewed and the interview was conducted with the person mainly responsible for their care. Sometimes interviews were carried out jointly with the disabled person and the carer. If the disabled person was not able to answer questions about financial matters because they did not normally deal with their own financial affairs, help was sought from whoever was in the best position to provide this kind of information. When informaton was required from someone else the disabled person's permission was sought whenever practicable.

Interviews were achieved with 80% of the disabled adults selected for interview; a further 9% were not interviewed either because they no longer had the disability recorded at the screening stage or because the disabled person had died, entered an institution or was too disabled to be interviewed and no-one else was available to be interviewed on their behalf. Non-response for this reason was more common when the initial screening had been carried out by post because of the interval of three to six months between the screening and the interview stage. When the screening was carried out by an interviewer interviews were arranged as soon after the screening call as possible. In only 11% of cases was there complete non-response at the interview stage. Table 5.2 gives details of the response at the interview stage.

Reference
[1] Wilson, P and Elliot, D (1987). The evaluation of the Postcode Address File as a sampling fame and its use within OPCS. *J. R. Statist. Soc.* Series A, Vol 150, Part 3.

Table 5.2 Response at the interview stage: disabled adults in private households

| | Method of screening: | | | | | |
| | Postal | | Interviewer | | Total | |
	No.	%	No.	%	No.	%
Adults to be interviewed:	14,440	100	3,529	100	17,969	100
Total interviewed	**11,484**	**80**	**2,824**	**80**	**14,308**	**80**
Full	8,248	57	2,231	63	10,479	58
Incomplete	470	3	86	2	556	3
All eligible for full interview	**8,718**	**60**	**2,317**	**66**	**11,035**	**61**
Short	2,766	19	507	14	3,273	18
Not interviewed	**2,956**	**20**	**705**	**20**	**3,661**	**20**
Temporary condition	1,222	8	81	2	1,303	7
Deceased/in institution/too ill	306	2	88	2	394	2
Non-contact	791	6	210	6	1,001	6
Refusal	637	4	326	9	963	5

Postal screening questionnaire

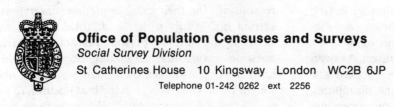

Office of Population Censuses and Surveys
Social Survey Division
St Catherines House   10 Kingsway   London   WC2B 6JP
Telephone 01-242 0262 ext 2256

Survey number
S1192/3

SURVEY OF DISABILITIES AND HEALTH PROBLEMS

Dear Sir or Madam

We are asking for your help with a survey. We have been asked by the Department of Health and Social Security to do a survey to find out about adults and children in Great Britain with disabilities, health problems or the kind of difficulties which are common in old age. The survey will help to develop policies for services and benefits for people with disabilities and their families.

We are contacting a random selection of addresses chosen from a list of all the addresses in the country. Your address is one of the ones chosen. We would like you to help by filling in this form about all the people living in your household. It will not take very long.

We are particularly interested in any problems people have doing ordinary everyday things because of disabilities, health problems or just because of old age. It is just as important for us to know how many people do not have any difficulties as it is to find out how many do. So please fill in the form about **everyone** in your household, including children, **even if no-one has any difficulties.**

EVERYONE'S ANSWER IS IMPORTANT

As in all our surveys we rely on people's voluntary co-operation. The information that you give is treated in strict confidence by OPCS. It is not released to any other Government department in any way in which it can be associated with your name or address. No information about you or anyone in your household is ever passed to members of the public or press. In published reports the identity of an individual is never revealed; the results of the survey are shown as statistics only.

Thank you for helping us with the survey.

Yours sincerely

Jean Martin

Jean Martin
Principal Social Survey Officer

If *no-one lives permanently* at the address at the top of the page, please tick one of the boxes below.

Address is vacant	1
Address is used for business purposes only	2
Other address where no-one lives permanently (eg holiday home, school)	3

If the address is an institution *with permanent residents*, please tick box and fill in details below.   4

Name of institution _____

Type of institution (eg hotel, old people's home) _____

Number of **permanent** residents _____ _____

PTO

Please answer the questions about everyone in your household

Include anyone who is temporarily away (for example in hospital or at school) but exclude anyone who lives somewhere else permanently.

1. How many people (men, women and children) are there in your household living at this address (including yourself)?

NUMBER

Total number of people in the household ☐

2. Please will you list below the ages and sex of everyone in your household.

AGE (in years - enter 0 for babies under 1 year)	SEX (Please tick) Male	Female		AGE (in years - enter 0 for babies under 1 year)	SEX (Please tick) Male	Female
Person 1. ☐	☐	☐	Person 6. ☐	☐	☐
Person 2. ☐	☐	☐	Person 7. ☐	☐	☐
Person 3. ☐	☐	☐	Person 8. ☐	☐	☐
Person 4. ☐	☐	☐	Person 9. ☐	☐	☐
Person 5. ☐	☐	☐	Person 10. ☐	☐	☐

3. Is any part of the address shown on the label overleaf, *separately* occupied by persons not entered above?

TICK ONE BOX   Yes ☐   No ☐

Please answer each of the following questions by ticking the Yes box if it applies to anyone in your household and ticking the No box if it does not apply to anyone.

4. Does anyone in your household have the following difficulties due to long-term health problems or disabilities, either physical or mental?

Yes   No

(a) Difficulty walking for a quarter of a mile on the level ☐ ☐

(b) Great difficulty walking up or down steps or stairs ☐ ☐

(c) Difficulty bending down and straightening up, **even** when holding on to something ☐ ☐

(d) Falling or having great difficulty keeping balance ☐ ☐

(e) Difficulty using arms to reach and stretch for things ☐ ☐

(f) Great difficulty holding, gripping or turning things ☐ ☐

(g) Difficulty recognising a friend across the road, **even** if glasses or contact lenses are worn ☐ ☐

(h) Difficulty reading ordinary newspaper print, **even** if glasses or contact lenses are worn ☐ ☐

(i) Difficulty hearing someone talking in a quiet room ☐ ☐

(j) Severe suffering from noises in the head or ears ☐ ☐

43

			Yes	No
(k)	Difficulty going outside the house or garden without help		☐	☐
(l)	Great difficulty following a conversation if there is background noise, for example, a TV, radio or children playing		☐	☐

5. **Is there anyone in your household who is affected by the following health problems or disabilities?**

		Yes	No
(a)	Severe and frequent bouts of breathlessness, wheezing or coughing which limit daily activities	☐	☐
(b)	Severe difficulties with eating, drinking or digestion which limit daily activities	☐	☐
(c)	Severe pain or irritation which limits daily activities	☐	☐
(d)	A scar, blemish or deformity which limits daily activities	☐	☐
(e)	Lack of control of bladder at least once a day or night	☐	☐
(f)	Lack of control of bowels at least once a month	☐	☐

6. **Does anyone in your household have the following long term health problems or disabilities?**

		Yes	No
(a)	A fit or convulsion in the past two years	☐	☐
(b)	Difficulty being understood by other people	☐	☐
(c)	Difficulty understanding what others say or what they mean	☐	☐
(d)	Frequently getting confused or disorientated	☐	☐
(e)	Severe depression or anxiety	☐	☐
(f)	Difficulty getting on with people, so that family life, work or leisure is severely affected	☐	☐
(g)	Mental handicap or other severe learning difficulties	☐	☐
(h)	Mental illness or phobias which limit daily activities	☐	☐

7. **In the last twelve months has anyone in your household seen a psychiatrist or other specialist *because of a mental, nervous or emotional problem*?** ☐ ☐

8. **In the last twelve months has anyone in your household attended a day centre, taken sheltered work or lived in sheltered housing *because of a health problem or disability*?** ☐ ☐

9. **Has anyone in your household attended a special school *because of a long-term health problem or disability*?** ☐ ☐

PTO

10. **Is there anyone in your household who, because of a long-term health problem or disability** . . . .

Yes   No

(a)   Would find it difficult to live alone without help?

(b)   Is dependent on life-sustaining equipment?

Yes   No   Retired

(c)   Is limited in the type or amount of paid work they can do?

These questions are about all children under 16 (including babies and toddlers) in your household. If there are no children go on to question 12

11.   **Is there any child in your household**

Yes   No

(a)   who is unable to do things which most children of the same age can do, because of a health, development or behaviour problem?

(b)   who needs more help than usual for children of the same age with feeding, dressing, toileting, walking, going up and down stairs or other daily activities?

(c)   who attends a special school, or special or remedial unit of an ordinary school, because of health or behaviour problems, disabilities or learning difficulties?

(d)   who attends an ordinary school but is limited in taking part in school activities because of health or behaviour problems or disabilities?

(e)   whose health, behaviour or development causes worry that he or she may have a long term health problem, physical or mental disability or handicap?

---

12.   **Does anyone (including any child) in your household have other difficulties with daily activities because of disabilities or long term health or behaviour problems not mentioned so far?**   Yes   No

PLEASE DESCRIBE . . . .

. . . .

13.   **If you have ticked any of the Yes boxes please complete the following details about everybody with the difficulties or problems mentioned:**

NAME (Please print)	SEX (Please tick) Male Female	DATE OF BIRTH Day Month Year	HEALTH PROBLEM OR DISABILITY (Please describe)
1.			. . . .
2.			. . . .
3.			. . . .
4.			. . . .

SOC(T)9c 5/85

6 Design of the survey of adults living in communal establishments

6.1 Introduction

The design of the survey of adults living in communal establishments differed from the corresponding private household survey in several key respects:

(i) To obtain a sample of disabled adults in establishments, a sampling frame had to be found or constructed that included all such establishments and omitted, as far as possible, private households. It was then necessary to screen these establishments to identify those which catered for permanently resident adults, that is any adults who would have been excluded from the private household survey.

(ii) It was assumed that all permanent residents in establishments had some degree of disability.

(iii) The administration of an interview schedule within an establishment required different procedures from those used in the private household survey. Procedures had to be developed to obtain information about individuals many of whom were likely to be aged and have reduced mental faculties. Such characteristics also affected the design of the interview schedule in terms of both content and structure.

This chapter describes the sampling frame and the selection of establishments for the survey, the selection of individuals within establishments and the various procedures which were adopted to obtain completed interviews.

6.2 Obtaining a sample of institutions

A list of institutions held by Vital Statistics Branch of the Population Statistics Division of OPCS was used as the sampling frame. The list, which is computerised and regularly updated, is used for coding the place of a birth or a death if it occurs outside a private household. It has approximately 20,000 entries covering all institutions in England and Wales. The adequacy of the coverage was checked by comparing entries in this list with other lists that were available from the DHSS and local authorities. This validation exercise demonstrated the OPCS list of institutions to have excellent coverage for institutions catering for adults. Institutions are listed in alphabetical order within a 42-fold classification of type of institution, within registration district and within region. The 42-fold typology is subsumed under six high-order groups—hospitals, educational establishments, homes, places of detention, military establishments, and other communal establishments. The classification of institutional type is shown in Table 6.1. For the purpose of the survey, hospitals, homes and hostels (both state-run and private) were included, and

Table 6.1 Classification of institution type

Hospitals	
	11 NHS medical
	12 NHS psychiatric
	13 NHS geriatric
	14 NHS mixed
	15 Private medical
	16 Private psychiatric
	17 Private geriatric
	18 Private mixed
	19 Schools attached to hospitals
Educational	
	21 Universities
	22 Polytechnics
	23 Residential teacher training (not polytechnic)
	24 Residential adult education
	25 Residential 'other' further education (including art colleges)
	26 Boarding schools
	27 Residential special schools (not 19)
	28 Halls of residence (not attached to above)
Homes	
	31 Non-private children (including residential)
	32 Non-private old persons
	33 Non-private disabled
	34 Private children (including nurseries)
	35 Private old persons
	36 Private disabled
	37 Hostels not assignable
Places of detention	
	41 Prisons
	42 Borstals
	43 Approved schools
	44 Establishments for criminally insane
	45 Remand centres
Military establishments	
	51 Self-contained—British
	52 With external accommodation—British
	53 Foreign
	54 Military colleges (not 52)
	55 Schools for children of service men
	56 Military hospitals (not 51)
Other communal	
	91 Convents and monasteries
	92 Social services hostels (for ex-prisoners etc)
	93 Part III accommodation
	94 Nurses homes not attached to hospitals
	95 'Doss' houses—identifiable (otherwise 96)
	96 Private hostels (YMCA etc)
	97 Others

educational establishments, places of detention and military establishments were excluded. Similar inclusion and exclusion criteria were applied to an equivalent list kept by the General Register Office for Scotland which was then appended to the list for England and Wales.

In order to get an adequate representation of institutional types and sizes it was estimated that five hundred to seven hundred institutions were required. Initially double the estimated maximum number (1,408) were contacted which represented a sampling fraction of 1 in 13 of our compiled list of institutions.

The main reason for writing to the establishment was to distinguish those with permanent residents from those

46

with no permanent residents at all. Only 'permanent residents' of institutions were of interest because 'non-permanent' residents were included in the population covered in the private household survey at their household address. A permanent resident was defined as:

'Anyone (excluding staff and their families) aged 16 or over, who:

(a) had been permanently resident in the establishment for the last six months, *or*

(b) had been resident in the establishment for less than six months, *but*

   (i) had been in residential care anywhere for at least six months, *or*

   (ii) had no other place of residence than this establishment at this time, *or*

   (iii) although having another place of residence, was expected to remain in residential care for the foreseeable future.'

The reasons for writing to more institutions than it was intended to have in the sample were:

(i) to get an adequate representation of the very large institutions which we knew would be greatly out-numbered by smaller ones;

(ii) to allow for ineligible institutions: those with no permanent residents (eg maternity hospitals) or those with fewer than four permanent residents or those that had changed their function or closed down, and

(iii) to allow for refusals and non-contacts.

A detailed breakdown by type of the 1,408 institutions initially contacted by letter is shown in Table 6.2.

Table 6.2   Number of different types of institutions contacted

Type of institutions contacted	Number contacted
Aged person's homes	481
Part III accommodation	342
Private nursing homes	127
General hospitals	100
Psychiatric hospitals or units	51
Geriatric hospitals or units	49
Establishments for mentally handicapped adults	26
Mental hostels (mentally ill)	25
Chronic sick hospitals or units	19
Maternity hospitals	15
Hostels	14
Homes for the blind	10
Others (fewer than 10 contacted):	
Aged person blind homes	
Cheshire homes	
Deaf homes	
Disabled persons homes	
Holiday homes	
Homes for the physically handicapped	
Medical nursing homes	
Mental after-care homes	
Monasteries	
Reception centres	
Rehabilitation centres	
Temporary accommodation for those in need	
Unmarried mothers homes	
Welfare institutes	
YMCA and YWCA	

6.3 Selection of institutions for the survey

The response from the postal inquiry to the 1,408 institutions is shown in Table 6.3. A total of 892 institutions (63%) were found to be eligible (that is had four or more permanent residents and were willing to co-operate in a future survey). A further 20 establishments were also willing to co-operate but had to be ruled out as they had fewer than four permanent residents.

The establishments with no permanent residents were predominantly maternity hospitals, general hospitals catering for short stay acute admissions, holiday homes and some religious establishments (convents and monasteries).

Table 6.3   Response from postal inquiry to establishments

	No.	%
Co-operating establishments (4 or more permanent residents)	892	63
No permanent residents	140	10
Refusals	133	9
Establishments closed down	64	5
Ineligible establishments	38	3
Non-contacts (including cases of information obtained too late)	141	10
Total	1,408	100

6.4 Selection of individuals within each institution

The 892 eligible co-operating institutions were then listed in descending order of the number of permanent residents. It was decided to use a sampling design that gave every institution, irrespective of the number of permanent residents it contained, an equal chance of selection. This meant we would have a variable number of interviews carried out at each institution. The final part of the sampling design was as follows:

(i) One third of the 892 institutions was randomly rejected (leaving a sample of 595 institutions).

(ii) When the number of permanent residents in the institution was 80 or less, *one in four* residents was selected for interview.

(iii) When the number of permanent residents in the institution was 81 or more, *one in twelve* residents was selected for interview.

The data obtained from interviews in large establishments has been weighted so that results are representative of residents in all establishments irrespective of size.

It was estimated that this sampling design would produce approximately 4,000 interviews in the 595 institutions. Because each institution had to have a minimum of four permanent residents there would have to be at least one interview per institution.

Table 6.4 shows that twenty-five establishments, although agreeing to co-operate on the survey, were ineligible. These were mainly sheltered accommodation. Each flat was individually numbered and had a separate address, thus making it eligible for the private household survey. Thirteen establishments decided to withdraw at this stage; about half changed their minds and half said the initial response to co-operate was given by someone who did not have the authority to give permission in the first place. Thus, interviewing took place in 570 establishments.

Table 6.4 Establishments' response to the survey

	No.	%
Fully co-operative	570	96
Establishments withdrawn:		
Ineligible	10	2
Refusals (change of mind)	7	1
Refusals (person in charge had not given permission originally)	6	1
Closed down	2	0
Total withdrawn	25	4
Original sample of establishments	595	100

The sampling procedure can be summarised as follows:

Institutions in OPCS and GRO (Scotland) lists

22,000 (approx)

Omit:
Places of detention
Military establishments
Educational
establishments

18,295

Sample 1 in 13 — Stratified by region, area and type, with alphabetical listing of establishment within type

1,408

Letter to administrator asking for co-operation and number of permanent residents — Losses caused by: non-co-operation non-contact ineligible in response to letter

892

Listed in ascending order of number of permanent residents — Systematically de-select one third

592

Interviewers list permanent residents at establishments — Losses caused by: non-co-operation, ineligibles at the institutions

570

Achieved sample of institutions

6.5 Pilot surveys

Before the main-stage fieldwork was carried out two pilot surveys were undertaken. The first pilot survey was carried out in March 1986 in 12 establishments. The purpose of this pilot was to elicit the best procedures for arranging interviews and to examine the extent to which the corresponding private household questionnaires could be used for respondents in residential care. The main finding was that the private household schedules were inappropriate, mainly because many of the interviews had to be done with proxy informants. The questionnaire was therefore re-designed to be more suitable for proxy informants but allowing for individual residents to answer the questions if they were capable of doing so.

Thirty-six establishments were selected to take part in the second pilot survey and 35 co-operated. They were selected to reflect the widest possible range of type and size of establishment. The decision not to do an initial sift of all the permanent residents at the establishments was vindicated as practically all selected respondents had some degree of disability.

In terms of questionnaire structure and question wording, the results of the pilot indicated that:

(a) It was difficult to get a complete medical history. Even in hospitals and aged persons homes staff tended to know about recent complaints or illnesses but not long-standing illnesses.

(b) Proxy informants did not know everything about the subject and certain questions referred to activities which could not be assessed, either because they were not in the behavioural repertoire of the subject or the institution, or the subject was too disabled for an assessment to be made.

(c) The proxy informant's knowledge of the financial affairs of the subject was often quite limited.

(d) Several proxy informants needed to be approached to complete a schedule for one subject. Knowledge of what the subject can and can't do, use of services, and management of finances, may reside with different individuals.

In terms of questionnaire administration the results of the pilot highlighted the distinction between a subject's ability to give permission for the survey to take place and his or her competence to answer the questions in the schedule. Whenever possible the subject's permission was sought. Special consideration was given to financial questions. Proxy informants were only asked about the management of the subject's financial affairs when they had some degree of responsibility for them.

6.6 Interviewing procedures

Many permanent residents in institutions are not capable of answering questions, especially detailed questions in an interview schedule. This inability may be due to age, ill-health and/or lack of interest that often accompanies institutionalisation.

It was not possible to give precise instructions to interviewers indicating who should or should not be interviewed. Both the wishes of the administrator and the experience of the interviewer were taken into account in making the decision of who would be interviewed.

The arrangements that were made for carrying out the interviews also varied. In some cases a member of staff sat in on the interview with the subject; in other cases the administrator was interviewed on behalf of all subjects even though they were competent to answer. In such cases the subject was given the opportunity to refuse. There were also some instances where the interview was split—the administrator answered some questions, the subject others.

Most permanent residents in institutions are there because they cannot look after themselves or have no one to look after them in private households. The majority tend to be elderly and in poor health. This affects their stamina for answering questions. Similarly detailed knowledge on various subjects and comprehension of concepts is limited. Thus the questionnaire had to be short with questions made as simple as possible.

When conducting interviews in institutions, interviewers were instructed to find a relatively private place and conduct the interview at a time that did not interfere with the routine of the place. The interviewers had to obtain permission from the relevant authorities not only to interview the subject but also to interview staff where appropriate so as not to interfere with their work.

6.7 Response to the interview

Response to the interview is shown in Table 6.5.

Table 6.5 Response to the interview: disabled adults in establishments

	No.	%
Full interviews	3,533	93
Short interviews		
Ineligible for full	213	6
Incomplete information	6	0
Subject left institution	13	0
Subject died	10	0
Total short interviews	242	6
Refusal	16	0
Total adults selected for interview	3,791	100

Subjects who left the establishment or who had died were retained in the analysis of the response to the interview because they were living in the establishment at the time of sampling. Subjects who were ineligible for full interview were those with no long term health problems; in such circumstances the majority of the questionnaire was inapplicable.

7 Defining disability and measuring severity

7.1 Introduction

Chapter 2 described the conceptual basis for the surveys and in particular the importance attached to the concept of disability as a continuum ranging from very severe to very slight. It was agreed very early on that the study should not attempt to cover the whole range of severity, but should identify a lower level above which people would be considered disabled for the purposes of the surveys and measure severity above this level. The screening stages represent successive moves towards the accurate identification of people at or above this level.

Chapter 2 also contained a brief account of the measures of severity developed for the study, in so far as this was necessary to understand the results presented in Chapters 3 and 4. This chapter gives a detailed account of the development of the measures and describes how the level of disability above which people were considered to be disabled was established.

7.2 The need for assessments of severity

We examined the literature for possible scales and different approaches to the problem of scaling severity of disability, but found no overall scale which covered a sufficiently wide range of disabilities to be adequate as comprehensive measure of severity for all types of disability. Many scales covered only disabilities resulting from physical problems and many were designed for use with an institutional population rather than for a survey of people living in private households. We were also concerned to base our measures on the ICIDH concept of disability and as yet no scale specifically linked to this classification has been developed. It was therefore decided to develop a measure specifically for the survey.

As the scale was intended to measure overall severity of disability, by which we mean the extent to which an individual's performance of activities is limited by impairments, we needed some means of getting from information about the particular activities people cannot perform to an assessment of their overall level of disability. There are three separate problems which cannot be solved by statistical analysis of the information collected in the interviews:

(a) Comparing the severity of specific limitations within an area of disability.

In some areas of disability the order of severity of particular limitations is obvious: not being able to walk is clearly more limiting than being able to walk only 50 yards. But in other areas the order of severity is not clear. For example, is not being able to wash oneself more limiting than not being able to get out of bed without help? Even if disabilities can be placed in order of severity, the distance apart in terms of severity cannot be determined by analysis of the interview data.

(b) Comparing the severity of disabilities in different areas.

The survey data provides no means of determining the relative severity of disabilities from different and unrelated areas. For example, is it more disabling not to be able to walk or not to be able to see, and by how much do these disabilities differ?

(c) Assessing the severity of combinations of disabilities.

The survey data also provides no means of deciding how combinations of disabilities should be treated. Should not being able to walk or see be considered to be a simple sum of the separate disabilities or should they be weighted in some way to allow for their interaction?

In order to compare different disabilities and to combine information about different disabilities into an overall measure we need a criterion of overall severity. Since the survey itself does not provide one, there is no satisfactory alternative to some form of judgement as the criterion of overall severity of disability. This could have taken the form of a research decision about how information about different disabilities should be combined into an overall measure, for example, that an overall measure could be obtained by simply summing the number of different activities an individual had difficulty with or could not perform. This decision involves two judgements: that the separate disabilities contribute equally to the overall measure and that the result is in fact a measure of overall severity.

We have adopted a more sophisticated approach in which assessments are used both to achieve a consensus about the meaning of overall severity of disability and to determine how the information from the survey about different disabilities should be combined to give an overall measure of severity. This approach relies on the judgements of people about the meaning of severity of disability. However, the procedures described below resulted in general agreement about what this is and about how the severity of individual disabilities contributes to the overall measure.

7.3 Summary of methods used

The methods used have been based on those used in the USA to develop a health status measure, the Sickness Impact Profile,[1] extended for use in this country on the Lambeth Survey of Disability.[2] As well as adapting this to our particular research needs, however, we have also introduced some substantial innovations.

The production of a single overall measure of severity of disability for each person interviewed on the survey involved five distinct stages, three of which used subjective, comparative judgements:

(a) Judgement of the relative severity of specific limitations within a single area of disability.

(b) Judgement of the relative severity of specific limitations across different areas of disability.

(c) Establishing a lower level of severity across all areas of disability above which people would be defined as disabled for the surveys.

(d) Judgements of the relative severity of combinations of specific limitations.

(e) Modelling how the judges assess different combinations of limitations and applying the model back to the survey respondents.

Initially each stage was tried out on staff in OPCS and DHSS connected with the surveys. Then we involved a range of professionals with expertise in disability—doctors from different specialities, physiotherapists, occupational therapists, psychologists and so on and people carrying out research in this area. People with disabilities and those caring for them and people from voluntary organisations concerned with disability were also involved.

Although the criterion of overall severity that we are using is based on a consensus of assessments of a large number of people acting as 'judges' and is therefore subjective, it is by no means arbitrary; the judges were given careful instructions and a high level of agreement in their assessments was achieved.

Nevertheless, any approach based on the use of subjective judgements as a criterion raises the problem of validation: how can it be shown that the measure devised for the survey actually measures what it is meant to measure? There is no easy answer to this question, since necessarily there is no objective criterion against which to validate the measure. As with many other measures of this kind validity is established by seeing how the measure works in practice. Does it have expected relationships with other variables? Do people placed at higher points on the scale seem to be more severely disabled than those at lower points? These kinds of questions will be answered partly through analysis of the survey data about people with disabilities and partly by other studies specifically designed to investigate the measure.

It is worth noting that there are many other well-established measures based on similar subjective criteria, for example many medical assessments, exam marks, particularly for essay style exams, and performance ratings used on staff appraisals in many organisations. But the common factor in all these assessments is that considerable efforts are made to train the assessors and to provide guidance on how the assessments are to be made to ensure that reliable results are obtained. Moreover, they are considered valid in so far as the people using them, both the assessors and those being assessed, consider them to be fair and valid; in most cases there is no objective external criterion against which they would be validated.

7.4 Initial selection of items for separate areas of disability

The first stage in constructing a scale of overall severity of disability was to carry out a considerable amount of multivariate statistical analysis to explore the relationships between the original areas of disability covered in the interview in order to reduce them to a more manageable number which could be presented to judges. Many of the original disabilities were interrelated and could be combined. For example, problems with walking, climbing steps and stairs, bending and balance are all covered in the locomotion area. Some of the original areas covered health problems or impairments rather than disabilities. As such they could be viewed as consequences of disability and so it would not be valid to include them in the main severity measure. It was therefore decided not to include information about them in the severity measures but to examine them separately.

Three areas of disability were not included at this stage, because the information collected in the interview did not give sufficiently specific descriptions of the disabilities. These were disabilities associated with suffering from fits or convulsions, problems with eating, drinking or digestion and having a scar, blemish or deformity. In the case of the first, a scale of severity of problems was developed after the scales for the other ten areas; for the second and third people were considered to be significantly disabled if such problems seriously affected their ability to lead a normal life, but no severity scales could be developed as there was insufficient information collected. All these problems are relatively uncommon and so we had had little information from pilot work on which to base more detailed measures.

Below we summarise the relationship between the original disability areas used in the interview and those for which separate severity measures were produced as a result of the rating exercises, and show the areas which were not included.

Original areas	Areas with separate scales
Included in rating exercises	
Walking	
Steps and stairs	Locomotion
Bending and straightening	
Falling and balance	
Reaching and stretching	Reaching and stretching
Holding, gripping and turning	Dexterity
Seeing	Seeing

Hearing	Hearing
Control of bladder and bowels	Continence
Being understood/understanding others	
	Communication
Self care and household activities	Personal care
Social behaviour and intellectual functioning	Behaviour
	Intellectual functioning

Added later

Fits and convulsions	Consciousness
Eating, drinking and digestion	Digestion
Disfigurement or deformities	Disfigurement

Excluded because impairment, not disability
Anxiety and depression
Breathlessness, wheezing and coughing
Pain or irritation

The criteria for selecting the particular items (limitations) to be used in each were:

(i) The items had to have been included on the survey. All the items used to filter people for the separate disability sections in the questionnaire were included.

(ii) We aimed to avoid selecting items that were highly correlated with one another, since we could impute a severity rating for any such items not included in the exercises.

(iii) Some areas included questions which formed a natural scale. In such cases we sometimes excluded some of these constituent questions and imputed values for them from others on this scale.

(iv) We needed to simplify the task for the judges. This meant we had to avoid including too many items in any one area, particularly if those items involved very small wording changes.

(v) Certain questions used in the survey deliberately aimed to be over-inclusive and therefore used a rather general or vague form of words. These items were excluded.

Applying these criteria to the selection process produced 134 items which were piloted in a first judgement exercise involving judges only from the participating departments, OPCS and DHSS. A number of other criteria were then applied to reduce this set still further.

(vi) A few items that were rated very inconsistently by different judges were excluded at this stage (but were incorporated later).

(vii) Where a number of items were rated similarly by judges, one or more of these were removed and their values imputed at a later stage.

This finally reduced the number of items to 99 divided between the ten areas.

7.5 Selection of judges

The broad aim of these judgement exercises was to attempt to identify any general consensus about the degree of limitation associated with different disabilities. This meant recruiting a range of people to act as judges, although we deliberately concentrated on people with some special involvement with the disability field, on the basis that they would have some knowledge or experience of the likely degree of limitation associated with different types of disabilities. Initially each judgement task was tried out on staff from OPCS and DHSS who had some interest in the survey. Later we recruited a range of professionals with appropriate expertise—doctors, physiotherapists, occupational therapists and psychologists, as well as independent researchers working in the area. Finally we approached a number of voluntary organisations concerned with disability and through them recruited disabled people and those caring for them to act as judges. Altogether about 100 people were involved in at least one of the judgement exercises.

7.6 Conduct of the first judgement exercise

A total of 45 judges took part in the first stage: 17 staff members, 18 specialists and 10 disabled people or carers.

For each area the judges were handed a packet of cards, each containing a description of an activity that an individual could not do or had difficulty with. Examples in the locomotion area were:

'Can only walk a few steps without stopping or severe discomfort'

'Occasionally needs to hold on to something to keep balance'

The judges were carefully briefed to ensure that, as far as possible, they all had the same understanding of the nature of the tasks. The briefing emphasised a number of factors:

—the distinction between disability and its consequences for different individuals, that is the resulting handicap;

—that they should not think about what might be causing the disability or the prognosis;

—that they should not think about what sort of person might have the disability and in particular they should not consider a person's age;

—that they should consider the activity not simply in its own right but also the implications that an inability to perform an activity would have on similar activities; and

—that they should consider the impact the disability would have on a typical day and assume that there would be no one available to help with the activity.

The judges were first asked to read all the cards in the packet to gain a complete picture of the range of activities within that area of disability. Next they were asked to place the least limiting activity at point 1 on the scale and the most limiting at point 11. Finally they were asked to place the remaining cards at positions along the scale, so that the distances between the cards reflected their opinions of the relative differences in limitation between the activities. More than one card could be placed at a scale point and not every point had to be used. Once the judges had completed their ratings for one set of cards they would move on to the next area of disability and carry out the task in an identical way, but *independently of the previous one.*

7.6.1 Results from the first judgement exercise
The means and standard deviations of the 45 judges' ratings were calculated for each limitation in each area of disability. The means allowed each limitation to be given a score on a severity scale for each area. From the standard deviations the reliability of the different items could be assessed and a few items with very low reliability were eliminated at this stage. These items related to relatively uncommon problems such as the use of devices to control bowels or bladder. It is arguable whether they should have been considered at all as they are not strictly speaking disabilities. These items were later incorporated into the scales at the lowest point on the final scales, so that people with such disabilities would not be excluded.

Three measures of agreement between judges were calculated, each measuring a slightly different aspect of agreement, and on each measure the general level of agreement was very high. The measures enabled us to quantify the consensus among the judges and to identify and exclude any judgements which were clearly well out of line with those of most of the judgements in each individual area. We were also able to determine whether there was a consistent minority view or whether disagreements were randomly distributed.

Two of the measures were derived from the judges' standardised scores. Standardisation ensured that items rated less consistently by judges were given less weight in the measures than those marked consistently. A measure of bias was calculated as the average standardised score of the items in one disability area and was used to indicate the extent to which judges were consistently under- or over-rating items relative to the other judges. Bias would be high (positive or negative) if, for example, a judge tended to rate most of the items at one end of the scale. A measure of variability was calculated as the average squared standardised score and was used to indicate the extent to which a judge was scoring the items a long way from the mean. Finally the correlation between each judge's scores and the mean scores for each area of disability was calculated. This correlation would be low if a judge ranked the items in that area very differently from the ranking of the mean scores. These correlations ranged from .72 to .90, with an average of .81, showing a high level of agreement.

These three measures are unaffected both by the number of items in the disability area and the number of points on the scale. This meant that we could apply a consistent standard of agreement to all areas and between the different judgement exercises. Two different standards were set for each measure to identify the levels needed to exclude 5% and 10% of judgements overall. These levels were based on an examination of the distributions of each measure across all judges and disability areas. Judges were then excluded independently in each area if:

(a) any of their measures exceeded the 5% point, or

(b) any two of their measures exceeded the 10% point.

These common standard values, used throughout the judgement exercises, are given in Table 7.1 below.

Table 7.1 Standards for exclusion of judges' ratings

	5% point	10% point
Correlation	0.5	0.65
Bias	±0.75	±0.6
Variability	2.2	1.75

As a result of this, between three and six judges were excluded from the different areas of disability. Once this had been done, the means and standard deviations were recalculated for each item: the means were very little changed but the standard deviations were reduced as a consequence. There was no evidence of a consistent minority view among the judges who were excluded, nor were the same judges excluded in each of the different areas of disability.

7.6.2 Problems of the intellectual functioning scale
The first version of this scale resulted in very poor agreement among judges. On applying the criteria for eliminating judges to the intellectual functioning scale, 22 of the 45 judges would have needed to be eliminated, which was clearly unacceptable. For this reason another way was sought to scale this area.

Originally judges were asked to rate the relative severity of the intellectual items separately in the same way as the other areas. In view of the low level of agreement we reconsidered our approach and it was decided that the activities that a person with intellectual problems would have difficulty with were so highly correlated that people with a disability in this area would be likely to have difficulty with a range of the activities described and not just one. Judges were therefore asked to rate the severity of someone with all eleven of the intellectual limitations compared to someone with eight and with four of the limitations. The results were then re-analysed in the way described above and achieved a level of agreement comparable with those achieved in the other disability areas.

Analysis of these results suggested a linear relationship between the number of problems experienced and the average severity scores and we were therefore able to impute a score for any number of problems between one and eleven.

7.6.3 Validation of the ten disability area scales
The first scaling exercise resulted in ten separate scales. Within each area the mean ratings were used to determine the positions of each item on each scale. Finally, the items that were excluded because of their

53

relationship with other items were assigned values based on the preliminary analysis described above.

As one check on the validity of the severity scales for the ten areas, the corresponding survey data was used to carry out a principal component analysis for each area and to calculate scores on the first principal component. The average principal component score for people reporting each limitation provides an alternative means of scaling the limitations, based not necessarily on severity but more on the relative frequency of the limitations and their tendency to be reported together. Nevertheless we should expect a reasonably high correlation between the two scoring methods, with commoner disabilities on the whole being rated as less severe than rarer ones.

The correlations between the two sets of scores are shown in Table 7.2. Note that the intellectual functioning correlation applies to the original, abandoned scale; the revised scale does not allow this form of comparison.

Table 7.2 Correlations between alternative scoring methods

Type of disability	Correlation
Locomotion	.88
Reaching and stretching	.77
Dexterity	.81
Seeing	.95
Hearing	.95
Personal care	.74
Continence	.92
Communication	.87
Behaviour	.85
Intellectual functioning	(.19)

These very respectable correlations, as well as giving us confidence in our severity measure, convinced us that it was reasonable to assign disability area severity scores to people interviewed for the survey on the basis of just their most severe limitation in that area rather than seeking a more elaborate method of combining scores for people with more than one limitation in one area.

7.7 Conduct of the second judgement exercise

Once we had established the severity levels of disabilities within different areas, the next step was to compare disabilities from the different scales, that is across different areas of disability.

The items rated on average the most limiting and the least limiting in each of the ten areas from the first exercise were selected for this second step. Judges were asked to rate the severity of these 20 items on a 15-point scale. Point 1 was used to represent the least limiting activity, and point 15 the most limiting activity.

For this second judgement exercise we recruited 57 judges, of whom 18 were staff members, 15 were specialists and 24 were disabled people or carers. The extra emphasis placed on the views of disabled people at this crucial second stage reflected our belief that this was likely to be the most controversial part of the procedure

and the one where the judges were likely to show the least agreement.

As before, judges were carefully briefed. As well as the points covered in the previous exercise, they were asked to take account simultaneously of the differences in severity between the most and least severe limitations in each area and also the differences among the most and least severe limitations for the different areas, all using the 15-point equal interval scale.

7.7.1 Results from the second judgement exercise
As with the first exercise, we wanted to measure the consensus view of the judges, so the same standards were applied to identify and eliminate dissenting judges.

Considering the greater conceptual and procedural complexity of this second task it was remarkable that only seven of the 57 judges were eliminated as a result; about the same proportion as were eliminated from the earlier exercise. Again, those excluded did not represent a consistent minority view. Thus our earlier fears that no consensus might emerge proved to be unfounded.

From the mean scores of the most and least severe limitation for each area, it was a simple matter to calculate where all the intermediate limitations on each scale should be. Since the length of the final scale is arbitrary, we chose to rescale so that the least limiting item was scored 1 and the most limiting was scored 15 on the new common scale. The revised intellectual scale was incorporated later, resulting in an upper limit of 16, since the top of this scale was judged to be higher than any of the existing scales. The relative positions of all the items included or imputed at the first stage are shown in Figure 7.1. The reference numbers correspond to those for items in the final scales given at the end of the chapter.

7.7.2 Assessing disability resulting from epilepsy
In the interview questions had been asked of people who suffered from fits or convulsions to establish how disabling their problems were. This information was not included in the judgement exercises initially because it was thought that for relatively uncommon disabilities such as these it would be advantageous to consult people with direct knowledge and experience of the problems associated with epilepsy. However, a similar rating exercise was carried out on the basis of which a severity scale was developed. We have called this area 'consciousness' to indicate the sort of problems covered. The scale takes into account the frequency of fits, what time of day they occur, whether the person experiences a warning that they are about to have a fit and whether they actually lose consciousness. This scale is shown at the end of this chapter.

Once the severity scale had been established, items from the top and bottom of the scale were presented to judges together with some of the tops and bottoms of the other scales and judges were asked to rate the two new ones in relation to those that had already been rated. In this

Fig 7.1 Judges ratings of severity on a common scale

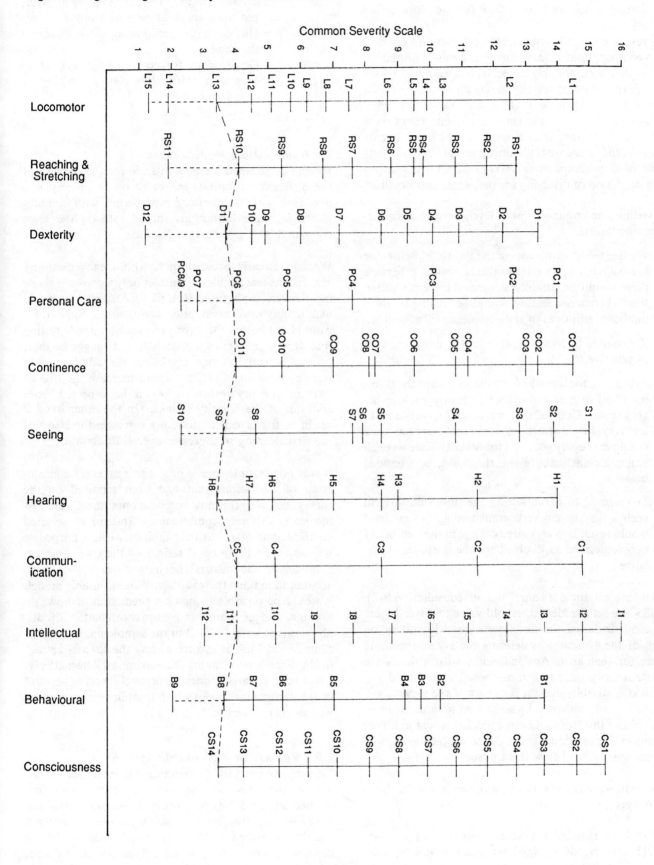

way the consciousness scale was integrated with the other scales.

7.8 Setting a common lower limit for disability across all areas

The results of the first two judgement exercises enabled us to compare limitations in different areas of disability. It was therefore possible to establish a common lower level or threshold of severity across all areas. So far as possible the questions used on the initial screening questionnaires and at the start of the interviews were intended to operate such a severity threshold, but of course at that stage we could only guess at the likely outcome of any comparative severity assessments so no final definition of disability for the survey was possible.

In setting the common lower level, several considerations pertained:

(a) We needed to avoid setting the threshold below the low values of the different area scales, otherwise there would be disabled people who were omitted from the survey and we would be unable to form unbiased estimates of the prevalence of disability.

(b) We wanted to retain as much of the interview data as possible.

(c) In practice the line which we drew to mark the threshold had to pass through one item on each of the area scales. Granted this, we wanted to avoid making very fine distinctions so limitations that were rated very nearly equal on the severity scale were all either included above the threshold, or excluded below it.

(d) We wanted to avoid setting the threshold level in such a way that a very small change in that level would result in a very large change in the number of people defined as disabled for the purposes of the survey.

Balancing all these factors and in consultation with DHSS, we set the ideal threshold value to 4 (see Figure 7.1), but included the next lower rated limitation on each of the 10 scales as defining the *actual* threshold value for that area. Any individual with a limitation whose severity was rated at or above the threshold was defined as disabled for the purposes of the survey, and conversely any individual who had no limitations rated at or above this threshold was excluded from the survey estimates. Approximately 5% of the people interviewed on the survey fell below this threshold.

The items which were excluded as being below the threshold were:

L14	Has fallen once or twice in the past year
L15	Needs to hold on occasionally to keep balance
RS11	Has difficulty raising one arm above the head to reach for something (but not the other arm)

D12	Can pick up and carry a 5 lb bag of potatoes with one hand but not with the other
PC7,8,9	Has difficulty washing hands and face, dressing and undressing, washing all over, but does not need help with any
S10	Has difficulty recognising a friend across the road
B9	Occasionally forgets to turn things off
I12	Has some difficulty reading, writing or calculating

7.9 Combinations of disabilities

Having established a common scale for the severity of the different limitations measured on the survey, the next task was to determine how people with combinations of these limitations should rate on the scale compared with people with just one.

We had already decided that, within each disability area, it was reasonable to consider only a person's single most severe limitation. However we wanted to avoid making any prior assumption across areas. Similarly it would have been quite wrong to assume without testing that disabilities were simply additive. It might be that, once a person has one disability, the addition of a second, different disability would increase the overall level of severity less than would be expected from addition of the severity ratings. On the other hand it might be that a second disability enhances the effect of the first, leading to a greater overall disability.

It was not feasible to ask judges to rate every combination of limitations that had been reported on the survey, nor even the most common ones: there were just too many different combinations. Instead we selected combinations of up to four limitations in a purposive way and used the judges' ratings of these to construct a model of the factors the judges were taking into account in making their ratings. With a suitable model, it would be possible to make a prediction of how, on average, judges would rate any combination of disabilities that an individual in the sample might have. A simple model might involve adding the severity ratings of the disabilites or taking the maximum. Alternatively, a more complicated model might involve taking account of the particular areas in which disabilities occurred, as well as their severity.

7.9.1 The selection of disability profiles

To simplify the task of selecting combinations of disabilities for this exercise, the limitations were first formed into three severity groups. Limitations rated less than 8 were termed 'appreciable'; those rated from 8 but less than 12 were termed 'severe'; and those rated 12 or more were termed 'very severe'. Secondly the ten areas of disability were divided broadly into physical, mental and sensory problems. 'Profiles' comprising two, three or four limitations were selected to represent the various combinations of severity bands and types of disabilities.

As far as possible the profiles comprising three and four disabilities were formed by taking previously selected combinations of two or three disabilities and in each case adding a different third or fourth. By combining two, three and four disabilities in this way, the extent to which adding another problem to a combination affects the severity of that combination can be examined.

Although the selected profiles were not a random sample of all profiles, only combinations of disabilities which occurred in the sample were used.

In all we selected 44 profiles of two disabilities, 22 profiles of three disabilities and 18 profiles of four disabilities.

7.10 Conduct of the third judgement exercise

For this, the final judgement exercise, a larger number of judges was recruited, since we anticipated a wider divergence of views than we had observed at the earlier judgement exercises. A total of 80 judges was used: 29 staff members, 34 specialists and 17 disabled people.

In addition to the profiles of two, three and four limitations, judges were asked to rate two single limitations chosen from near the top and bottom of the severity scale. 'Cannot tell by the light where the windows are' was previously rated as the most severe limitation on the seeing scale and 'cannot walk 400 yards without stopping or severe discomfort' was rated the least limiting item of the locomotion scale. Asking judges to rate the single limitations relative to multiple limitations in this way provided the necessary link between this and the earlier rating exercises.

As in the previous exercise, judges were asked to rate the profiles on a 15-point scale of severity. Because of the large number of profiles involved, they were divided into two groups with most of the judges being asked to rate only one group.

To help judges assess the relative severity of the numerous combinations, an indication was given on each card, of the severity group of each separate limitation: A, S, or VS denoting appreciable, severe and very severe. However the judges did not have to take account of these earlier assessments if they did not agree with them.

Once again we asked the judges to read all the profile cards first, to get an idea of the range of combinations before placing any on the scale. They were asked to place their judgements of the least and more severely limiting profiles at scale points 1 and 15 respectively and the remaining cards were then positioned along the scale in relation to these.

7.10.1 Results from the third judgement exercise

As with the previous exercises, we wanted to measure the consensus view of the judges, so the same standards were applied to identify and eliminate dissenting judges.

As expected, a higher proportion of judges was eliminated at this stage, 17 of the original 80, leaving 63. However, there was no evidence of consistent minority views among the judges that were eliminated.

Profiles which included one of the two single limitations must logically be rated at least as severe as those single limitations. A few judges were found not to have done this and so their judgements of just these profiles were excluded before the means were calculated.

Having removed these inconsistent ratings, the mean ratings of the two single limitations were calculated and the average profile ratings were rescaled to make them commensurate with the previous single disability severity scale. This rescaling could have been achieved in a different way by using each judge's ratings of the single disabilities to rescale his/her own profile ratings, but it was felt that the former method would be more robust and in practice the two methods produced almost identical scales.

Another form of group inconsistency became apparent at this point. For a few profiles, the rescaled mean rating given to a combination of limitations was lower than one or more of the scale values of its constituent limitations. In such cases the profile rating was set to the maximum severity value of these limitations.

7.11 Models for disability profiles

Before attempting to model the processes used by the judges to determine appropriate severity scores for combinations of limitations, the profile and individual limitation scores were once again rescaled so that a score of 1 corresponded to the ideal threshold level. They were then rounded to the nearest .5 to produce the final disability scores given at the end of the chapter.

Since the profiles used for building models were not a probability sample of those found in the survey but rather were selected to enable certain types of model to be compared, we cannot strictly describe the process we used as statistical modelling. Nevertheless, we have borrowed the methods used by statistics to determine the values for model parameters and to measure goodness of fit. This is perfectly valid so long as we do not make use of statistical significance testing.

In comparing different models we made use of two criteria. The first, the correlation between the fitted and actual scores, can, when squared, be interpreted as the proportion of the variance between the scores that is explained by the model. A second, simpler measure, the 'error rate', is the proportion of profiles where the difference between the predicted and actual severity score exceeds two. The value two was chosen since the final scale was to be divided into no more than ten equal intervals: errors of one point on this scale are unavoidable however good the model, but we wanted to minimise the proportion of errors exceeding one point.

The models were fitted using least-squares regression through the origin. The simplest model we examined was based on the sum of the severity scores for the disabilities in the profile. This model produced a correlation of .910 but an error rate of 42%. An examination of the pattern of residuals showed it to be fitting the middle range of severity scores well but not the extremes. This suggested that a model which differentially weighted the more severe disabilities relative to the less severe should be tried.

We therefore fitted a linear regression model to the individual disability scores, ranked in decreasing order of severity. The coefficient of the most severe disability was fixed at one, so that the model could be applied to cases with a single disability without amendment. This produced a correlation of .966 and a much reduced error rate of 12%. We also fitted models to just the most severe two and three disabilities, to see if judges were using all the data in assessing severity. The two-factor model produced a correlation of .948 and an error rate of 18% and the three-factor model values of .964 and 13% respectively. We concluded that the third most severe disability was important but the fourth was not. Finally we rounded the fitted coefficients thus producing a model:

worst + 0.4(second worst) + 0.3(third worst)

We next examined whether adding further factors which identified the particular areas of disability would improve the already very good fit. Such factors improved the model very little; although some high residuals were reduced, an equal number were induced. The best additional factor identified cases whose two most severe disabilities were physical, but although this increased the correlation slightly to .965 and reduced the error rate to 11%, we felt that this gain was insufficient to justify an extra factor and that such a model would be less robust than the very simple one given above.

A summary of the fitted models is given in Table 7.3.

Table 7.3 Profile models and goodness of fit measures

	Correlation	Error rate
Model selected:		
Weighted worst 3	.964	13%
Other models tried:		
Simple sum	.910	42%
Weighted worst 4	.966	12%
Weighted worst 2	.948	18%
Weighted worst 3 + 2 physical	.965	11%

7.11.1 Application of the model to the disabled sample
To apply this model to a particular disabled adult in the survey one first has to find their three highest severity scores from the thirteen areas of disability (the original ten plus consciousness, digestion and disfigurement). For people with only one or two disabilities in different areas, the remaining scores are set to zero. Finally one combines the three severity scores according to the three-factor model:

worst + 0.4(second worst) + 0.3(third worst)

to produce a single severity score in the range 0.5 to 21.4.

For the purpose of providing estimates and analysing the survey data, severity scores need to be grouped into a number of discrete categories. From the outset it had been envisaged that between six and ten equal bands of severity would be appropriate. The advantage of the larger number is that, depending on the analysis required, either the full set of ten can be used or adjacent categories can be combined to give five—still sufficient for examining many trends associated with severity.

It is also advantageous to divide the scale in such a way that the natural peaks in the distribution are smoothed out. Peaks occur for scores which are whole numbers or 0.5, since these are the only scores possible for people with just one disability. The choice of ten, rather than six or eight categories gives an equal number of such peaks in each category.

Since each category has a severity score range of 2, the error rates quoted above give an indication of the proportion of the profiles which would have been assigned to a different category by the judges from that predicted from the model. However, we cannot simply apply this rate to the people on the survey, since the profiles contained higher proportions of multiple disabilities than found among the survey sample. Moreover, about 30% of individuals had only one disability and for these the issue of misclassification does not arise.

Careful attention needs to be paid to how the categories are described. There is no absolute meaning to terms such as 'very severe', 'severe' and so on. Thus to say 'The OPCS survey shows there are x thousand very severely disabled people in Great Britain' will have no meaning without a clear definition of 'very severely disabled'. It has therefore been decided to avoid the use of descriptive terms on their own and always to refer to the number of the severity category.

The final ten categories are as follows:

Severity category	Weighted severity score
10 (most severe)	19–21.40
9	17–18.95
8	15–16.95
7	13–14.95
6	11–12.95
5	9–10.95
4	7– 8.95
3	5– 6.95
2	3– 4.95
1 (least severe)	0.5– 2.95

In summary, to find a person's severity category:

(a) The scores associated with the first activity a person cannot do in each of the thirteen areas are found.

(b) The three highest non-zero scores are selected and summed applying the formula:

highest + 0.4(second highest) + 0.3(third highest)

(c) The severity category for the calculated severity score is determined from the table above.

It is worth noting that since the highest score for a single disability is 13, people in severity categories 8, 9 and 10 must necessarily have disabilities in more than one area. But people with multiple disabilities are not always found in the highest severity categories; it is possible to have three disabilities with low scores and to be in the bottom category.

Although the above scale has been used for analysis of the survey results, it has not yet been fully validated. The assignment of individuals on the survey to a severity category does not pose a problem, since it is determined by the rules given above. But, as mentioned above, there is no obvious external criterion against which the scale can be validated as a measure of severity of disability and so our general approach is to see how it performs in practice. Analysis of the survey results will show the extent to which it is correlated with other survey variables which might be expected to relate to severity of disability. Further research would need to be undertaken to examine its performance if it were to be used in other circumstances. It has been designed for use in the survey context and would need to be modified and validated for other uses, particularly if these were to involve the assessment of individuals rather than to provide a population measure.

References

1 Bergner *et al*. The sickness impact profile: conceptual formulation and methodology for the development of a health status measure. *International Journal of Health Sciences,* Volume 6. 1976.

2 (Lambeth Study) Health and care of the physically disabled in Lambeth Department of Community Medicine, St Thomas' Hospital Medical School.

The severity scales for areas of disability

LOCOMOTION   *Severity score*

L1   Cannot walk at all   11.5

L2   Can only walk a few steps without stopping or severe   9.5
     discomfort/Cannot walk up and down one step

L3   Has fallen 12 or more times in the last year   7.5

L4   Always needs to hold on to something to keep balance   7.0

L5   Cannot walk up and down a flight of 12 stairs   6.5

L6   Cannot walk 50 yards without stopping or severe discomfort   5.5

L7   Cannot bend down far enough to touch knees and straighten up   4.5
     again

L8   Cannot bend down and pick something up from the floor and   4.0
     straighten up again

L9   Cannot walk 200 yards without stopping or severe   3.0
     discomfort/Can only walk up and down a flight of 12 stairs if
     holds on and takes a rest/Often needs to hold on to something
     to keep balance/Has fallen 3 or more times in the last year

L10 Can only walk up and down a flight of 12 stairs if holds on   2.5
     (doesn't need a rest)

L11 Cannot bend down to sweep up something from the floor and   2.0
     straighten up again

L12 Can only walk up and down a flight of stairs if goes sideways   1.5
     or one step at a time

L13 Cannot walk 400 yards without stopping or severe discomfort   0.5

REACHING AND STRETCHING   *Severity score*

RS1 Cannot hold out either arm in front to shake hands   9.5

RS2 Cannot put either arm up to head to put a hat on   9.0

RS3 Cannot put either hand behind back to put jacket on or tuck   8.0
     shirt in

RS4 Cannot raise either arm above head to reach for something   7.0

RS5 Has difficulty holding either arm in front to shake hands with   6.5
     someone

RS6 Has difficulty putting either arm up to head to put a hat on   5.5

RS7 Has difficulty putting either hand behind back to put jacket on   4.5
     or tuck shirt in

60

REACHING AND STRETCHING—*continued*

RS8	Has difficulty raising either arm above head to reach for something	3.5
RS9	Cannot hold one arm out in front or up to head (but can with other arm)	2.5
RS10	Cannot put one arm behind back to put on jacket or tuck shirt in (but can with other arm)/Has difficulty putting one arm behind back to put jacket on or tuck shirt in, or putting one arm out in front or up to head (but no difficulty with other arm)	1.0

DEXTERITY

		Severity score
D1	Cannot pick up and hold a mug of coffee with either hand	10.5
D2	Cannot turn a tap or control knobs on a cooker with either hand	9.5
D3	Cannot pick up and carry a pint of milk or squeeze the water from a sponge with either hand	8.0
D4	Cannot pick up a small object such as a safety pin with either hand	7.0
D5	Has difficulty picking up and pouring from a full kettle or serving food from a pan using a spoon or ladle	6.5
D6	Has difficulty unscrewing the lid of a coffee jar or using a pen or pencil	5.5
D7	Cannot pick up and carry a 5lb bag of potatoes with either hand	4.0
D8	Has difficulty wringing out light washing or using a pair of scissors	3.0
D9	Can pick up and hold a mug of tea or coffee with one hand but not with the other	2.0
D10	Can turn a tap or control knob with one hand but not with the other/Can squeeze the water from a sponge with one hand but not the other	1.5
D11	Can pick up a small object such as a safety pin with one hand but not with the other/Can pick up and carry a pint of milk with one hand but not the other/Has difficulty tying a bow in laces or strings	0.5

PERSONAL CARE

Severity score

PC1   Cannot feed self without help/Cannot go to and use the toilet without help   11.0

PC2   Cannot get into and out of bed without help/Cannot get into and out of chair without help   9.5

PC3   Cannot wash hands and face without help/Cannot dress and undress without help   7.0

PC4   Cannot wash all over without help   4.5

PC5   Has difficulty feeding self/Has difficulty getting to and using the toilet   2.5

PC6   Has difficulty getting in and out of bed/Has difficulty getting in and out of a chair   1.0

CONTINENCE

Severity score

CO1   No voluntary control over bowels   11.5

CO2   No voluntary control over bladder   10.5

CO3   Loses control of bowels at least once every 24 hours   10.0

CO4   Loses control of bladder at least once every 24 hours   8.0

CO5   Loses control of bowels at least once a week   8.0

CO6   Loses control of bowels at least twice a month   6.5

CO7   Loses control of bladder at least once a week   5.5

CO8   Loses control of bowels at least once a month   5.0

CO9   Loses control of blader at least twice a month/Loses control of bowels occasionally   4.0

CO10   Loses control of bladder at least once a month   2.5

CO11   Loses control of bladder occasionally/Uses a device to control bowels or bladder   1.0

SEEING

		Severity score
S1	Cannot tell by the light where the windows are	12.0
S2	Cannot see the shapes of furniture in a room	11.0
S3	Cannot see well enough to recognise a friend if close to his face	10.0
S4	Cannot see well enough to recognise a friend who is an arm's length away	8.0
S5	Cannot see well enough to read a newspaper headline	5.5
S6	Cannot see well enough to read a large print book	5.0
S7	Cannot see well enough to recognise a friend across a room	4.5
S8	Cannot see well enough to recognise a friend across a road	1.5
S9	Has difficulty seeing to read ordinary newspaper print	0.5

HEARING

		Severity score
H1	Cannot hear sounds at all	11.0
H2	Cannot follow a TV programme with the volume turned up	8.5
H3	Has difficulty hearing someone talking in a loud voice in a quiet room	6.0
H4	Cannot hear a doorbell, alarm clock or telephone bell	5.5
H5	Cannot use the telephone	4.0
H6	Cannot follow a TV programme at a volume others find acceptable	2.0
H7	Difficulty hearing someone talking in a normal voice in a quiet room	1.5
H8	Difficulty following a conversation against background noise	0.5

COMMUNICATION

		Severity score
C1	Is impossible for people who know him/her well to understand/Finds it impossible to understand people who know him/her well	12.0
C2	Is impossible for strangers to understand/Is very difficult for people who know him/her well to understand/Finds it impossible to understand strangers/Finds it very difficult to understand people who know him/her well	8.5
C3	Is very difficult for strangers to understand/Is quite difficult for people who know him/her well to understand/Finds it difficult to understand strangers/Finds it quite difficult to understand people who know him/her well	5.5

C4   Is quite difficult for strangers to understand/Finds it quite difficult to understand strangers   2.0

C5   Other people have some difficulty understanding him/her/Has some difficulty understanding what other people say or what they mean   1.0

BEHAVIOUR

Severity score

B1   Gets so upset that hits other people or injures him/herself   10.5

B2   Gets so upset that breaks or rips up things   7.5

B3   Feels the need to have someone present all the time   7.0

B4   Finds relationships with members of the family very difficult   6.0

B5   Often has outbursts of temper at other people with very little cause   4.0

B6   Finds relationships with people outside the family very difficult   2.5

B7   Sometimes sits for hours doing nothing   1.5

B8   Finds it difficult to stir him/herself to do things/Often feels aggressive or hostile towards other people   0.5

INTELLECTUAL FUNCTIONING

	Severity score	*No of problems*
I1	13.0	11
I2	12.0	10
I3	10.5	9
I4	9.5	8
I5	8.0	7
I6	7.0	6
I7	6.0	5
I8	4.5	4
I9	3.5	3
I10	2.0	2
I11	1.0	1

Number of problems from the following:

Often forgets what was supposed to be doing in the middle of something

Often loses track of what is being said in the middle of a conversation

Thoughts tend to be muddled or slow

Often gets confused about what time of day it is

Cannot watch a half hour TV programme all the way through and tell someone what it was about

Cannot remember and pass on a message correctly

Often forgets to turn things off such as fires, cookers or taps

Often forgets the name of people in the family or friends seen regularly

Cannot read a short article in newspaper

Cannot write a short letter to someone without help

Cannot count well enough to handle money

CONSCIOUSNESS

	Severity score	Score
CS1	12.5	13.8
CS2	11.5	12.8–13.0
CS3	10.5	11.8
CS4	10.0	10.8
CS5	9.0	9.8–10.0
CS6	8.0	8.8–9.0
CS7	7.0	7.8–8.0
CS8	6.0	6.8–7.0
CS9	5.0	5.8–6.0
CS10	4.0	4.8–5.0
CS11	3.0	4.0
CS12	2.0	3.0
CS13	1.0	2.0
CS14	0.5	1.0

Add the scores for the following items:

Has fits:

Less than one year	0
Once a year but less than 4 times a year	1
4 times a year but less than once a month	2
Once a month but less than once a week	3
Once a week but less than every day	4
Every day	5
Only has fits during the night	1
Only has fits at the night or on awakening	3.8
Only has fits at the night, on awakening or in the evening	5.8
Has fits during the daytime	6.8
Always has a warning before a fit	0
Has fits without warning	1
Loses consciousness during a fit	1
Does not lose consciousness	0

EATING, DRINKING AND DIGESTION

Severity score

EDD1   Suffers from problems with eating, drinking or digestion which severely affects ability to lead a normal life   0.5

DISFIGUREMENT (Scars, blemishes and deformities)

Severity score

DF1   Suffers from a scar, blemish or deformity which severely affects ability to lead a normal life   0.5

8 Weighting to produce national estimates

8.1 Introduction

The primary aim of the disability surveys is to provide national estimates of the number of people defined as disabled for the purposes of the survey, by severity and type of disability for different age-groups. Chapter 7 described how we established the lowest level above which people were classified as disabled and the severity categories above this level. This enabled us to determine the numbers of adults on the two surveys in each severity band among those for whom complete interview information was available. This chapter outlines the methods used to obtain estimates from the surveys of the numbers of people in the population they represent and thus to provide both prevalence rates and population totals of the disabled, both overall and at different severity levels.

The two surveys of disabled adults were based on very different designs and this carries through to different methods of forming national estimates. This chapter describes the procedures used on each survey in turn. Despite the difference in methods, results from the two surveys can be added to give the whole picture for disabled adults in Great Britain. The way in which this has been done is described at the end of the chapter.

Two types of national estimate are included in this report. The first type, the *prevalence* estimate, is a rate of disability per thousand of the population. To form such estimates we need not only to estimate the total number of disabled people in the relevant section of the population, we also need a separate estimate of the total size of that section of the population.

Reliable estimates are not always available however. OPCS produces annual population estimates for England and Wales by updating census figures with births, deaths and net migration. Comparable population estimates are produced for Scotland by the General Registrar Office, Scotland. However these are subdivided only by age, sex, marital status and region. More detailed estimates from other sources, for example from other surveys, could be used but are subject to various kinds of errors, particularly sampling error and non-response bias. Thus prevalence rates based on such survey estimates would be subject to these additional sources of error, as well as those in the estimates from the disability surveys. For this reason, except for the particular case of ethnic minority groups, we have confined our prevalence estimates to the groups for which we have reliable total population estimates.

The second type of national estimate used in this report is the *total number* of disabled people in some section of the population. This type of estimate is not subject to the limitations of prevalence estimates noted above and so can be produced for a much wider range of groups in the population, in fact any reasonably large group that we can identify from the surveys.

8.2 Private household sample

A number of factors have to be taken into account in estimating national totals. Before discussing these, we summarise in Figure 8.1 the eight stages of the survey by which people with disabilities were identified. On the right are shown the factors which need to be taken into account in the estimation procedures. It should be noted that because the sift was conducted partly by post and partly by personal interview, the factors are handled separately for the two parts of the sample, although the principles for handling them remain the same.

Fig 8.1 Stages in the identification of people with disabilities from the general population

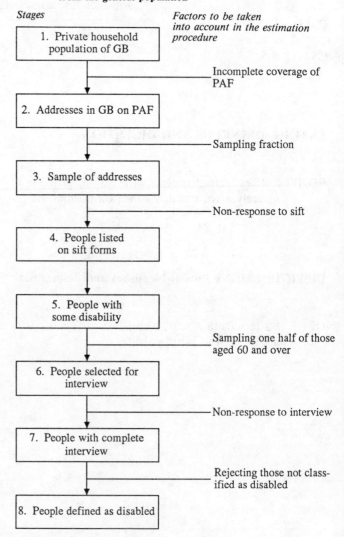

Stages	Factors to be taken into account in the estimation procedure
1. Private household population of GB	
	Incomplete coverage of PAF
2. Addresses in GB on PAF	
	Sampling fraction
3. Sample of addresses	
	Non-response to sift
4. People listed on sift forms	
5. People with some disability	
	Sampling one half of those aged 60 and over
6. People selected for interview	
	Non-response to interview
7. People with complete interview	
	Rejecting those not classified as disabled
8. People defined as disabled	

The basic idea is to produce a set of weights which can be applied to all disabled people interviewed in the survey. It is worth emphasising here that a number of people who completed a full interview did not meet our final criteria for being defined as disabled and so their data was not used in forming the national estimates.

In summary, the weights are required to gross to population totals, to allow for non-response at the sift and interview stages, for the disproportionate sampling of those aged 60 or over, and for people assumed to be disabled with whom no interview was possible.

Any attempt to correct non-response bias by weighting in this way is bound to be imperfect, depending as it does on the assumption that non-respondents are like some particular group of survey respondents. We have sought to mitigate this as far as possible by treating non-respondents not as a single homogeneous group, but instead as being like survey respondents in the same age group, with respect to disability. As a further precaution we have, as described in Chapter 5, followed up a one in ten sub-sample of addresses which failed to respond to the initial postal sift, which was the part of the sample with the lowest response rate. This allowed us to investigate the possibility of non-response bias with respect to disability at the postal screening stage.

The three basic steps required to convert a sample total of disabled people to a population estimate are as follows:

(a) Weight up the disabled people who had full interviews to represent those people who could not be interviewed for reasons which indicated that they definitely were disabled.

(b) Weight up all final interview respondents to represent all those people from the sift phase who were eligible for personal interview.

(c) Weight up all sift respondents to represent the total national population living in private households.

For the first two of these steps, people in addresses sifted by post or by an inteviewer were kept separate, since the proportion of people identified as potentially disabled by the different methods varied at both selection phases. The groups were combined for the third step since the division of the sample into the two method groups took place after the areas had been selected and so did not permit a corresponding division of the population to be made. For all three steps weights were calculated separately for 15 five-year age-groups.

These three steps are discussed in more detail below.

(a) Allowance for the disabled who could not be interviewed

Some people who were selected for interview were unable to be interviewed for reasons related to their disability. This includes those people who had died, entered an institution or who could not be interviewed because of ill health. It has been assumed that all such people would have been disabled and so disabled people who had full interviews (stage 8) are weighted up to represent them. There were 358 such people altogether.

This component of the weight varies between 1.03 and 1.12 for the different age-groups.

(b) Allowance for the under-sampling of the elderly and non-response to the interview

People with a complete final interview (stage 7) are weighted up to represent all those people from the initial screening phase who were eligible for a personal interview (stage 5).

This second component of the weight converts the respondents to the final interview (including the group not interviewed but allowed for in the previous step) to those people with some disability who were retained after the sift phase and therefore eligible for interview.

The weight compensates for two factors which resulted in a loss of people from the sample in moving from stage 5 to stage 7. First, half of the people aged 60 or over were not selected for a final interview and so the people in this age-group who remain must be given twice the weight of the younger people to compensate for this. Secondly, not all those people who were selected could be contacted or were willing to take part in the final stage of the survey, so those that remain must be weighted up to represent the non-respondents. The weight is simply the ratio of the number eligible for a final interview to the number responding. No attempt was made to assess non-response bias at this second phase. The component of the weight from this source varies between 1.07 and 1.43 for people aged under 60, and between 2.19 and 2.85 for people aged 60 and over.

(c) Allowance for non-response at the initial screening stage and for grossing from survey numbers to population totals

Population estimates show the composition of the total population in Great Britain with respect to age, sex and region. These estimates however include people not resident in private households, so they have been adjusted to the private household population using the rates applicable at the time of the 1981 Census. Because disability is known to be highly correlated with age and since too fine a breakdown increases the sampling error of the estimates, it was decided to use only the age distribution of the population as a control factor. Thus estimates are made separately for each of the 15 five-year age-groups.

The age of all people in the household was asked on the sift questionnaire. In practice some households gave incomplete answers at this question. For some households we know the number of people in the household but not their ages, whilst for others we do not even know the number of people. For such cases we have distributed the people across the different age-groups in the same proportions as for fully responding households and where necessary assumed that the average household size applies.

Weighting up the people listed on the sift forms (stage 4) to the total number of people living in private households in Great Britain (stage 1) allows for three different factors:

— the incomplete coverage of the sampling frame;

— the fact that we sampled only about one in 225 of the listed addresses;

— the non-response to the initial sift.

All these factors are simultaneously allowed for by completely bypassing the sampling frame and instead weighting directly to the population estimates. The components of the weight from this final step vary between 266 and 296 for the different age-groups.

We paid particular attention to non-response at the initial screening stage. Our concern was that disabled people might be more or less likely to respond than others. For this reason we undertook a special check on this part of the sample by following up a tenth of those addresses which did not respond initially, with a personal approach by an interviewer, as described in Chapter 5. This check provided no evidence that non-response was related to disability, once proper allowance had been made for the differences in the age distributions. On the basis of this, no further allowance for non-response was felt to be required.

The final weights, shown in Table 8.1, were applied to each of the five-year age bands for the samples screened by post and interviewers respectively. Results for each disabled adult interviewed on the survey were multiplied by the appropriate weight to obtain population estimates for Great Britain. In order to obtain prevalence rates, the population totals for the disabled were divided by estimates of the total number of people in the population in the relevant category.

Table 8.1 Combined weights for private household sample

Age-group	Sifted by post	Sifted by interviewer
16–19	377	322
20–24	456	401
25–29	372	405
30–34	380	333
35–39	359	316
40–44	350	316
45–49	360	296
50–54	330	343
55–59	412	363
60–64	614	607
65–69	708	728
70–74	701	726
75–79	755	723
80–84	810	722
85 and over	877	849

All the weights used to arrive at population estimates, with the exception of that required to gross from the sample to the total population, need to be applied to the survey results in presenting any analyses in order to obtain, as far as possible, unbiased sample distributions. When survey results are shown as percentages it is usual to show the number of cases on which percentages are based, to give a general impression of the reliability of the sample distributions for which sampling errors have not been calculated. However, the percentages are based not on the actual number of interviews but on the re-weighted figures which take account of non-response and under-sampling of those aged 60 or over. We have adjusted the weights so that the weighted total for the whole sample is 10,000, which is similar to the total of 10,561 disabled adults who were actually interviewed. Thus in any sample category, the real number of people in the sample may be greater or less than the weighted number shown but these will balance approximately overall. The alternative, to present actual sample numbers, would greatly distort the population distributions by under-representing elderly people.

8.3 Communal establishment sample

A rather different and in some ways simpler method of producing individual weights for disabled people was employed for this part of the survey. As before, we first summarise in Figure 8.2 the eight stages of the survey by which people with a significant level of disability were identified.

As with the private household sample, the weights used to produce national estimates are formed from three components:

— An allowance for the sampled adults who could not be interviewed.

— An allowance for the sampling within the selected establishments and non-response to the interview.

— An allowance for sampling and non-response of establishments.

(i) *Allowance for the sampled individuals who could not be interviewed*

A few individuals who were sampled had died before interviews could be obtained. It was assumed that such people were disabled and therefore the sample who were interviewed were weighted up to take account of them. This is identical to the first step used for the private household sample.

(ii) *Allowance for the sampling within the selected establishments and non-response to the interview*

People with a complete interview (stage 7) were weighted up to represent all permanent residents in the selected establishments (stage 5).

Again, two factors cause a loss of people from the sample in moving from stage 5 to stage 7. First, a quarter of the residents in small establishments but only a twelfth of those in large establishments were selected for interview, so people from large establishments must be given a larger weight.

Second, a small number of those selected for interview refused, so those interviewed must be weighted up to represent this group. This step amounts to multiplying the sampling fraction, 4 or 12, by the inverse of the response fraction.

Fig 8.2 Stages in the identification of people with disabilities in communal establishments

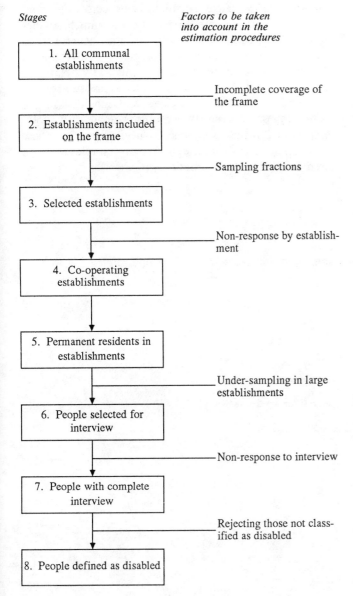

Stages

Factors to be taken into account in the estimation procedures

1. All communal establishments

— Incomplete coverage of the frame

2. Establishments included on the frame

— Sampling fractions

3. Selected establishments

— Non-response by establishment

4. Co-operating establishments

5. Permanent residents in establishments

— Under-sampling in large establishments

6. People selected for interview

— Non-response to interview

7. People with complete interview

— Rejecting those not classified as disabled

8. People defined as disabled

(iii) *Allowance for sampling and non-response of establishments*

Co-operating establishments (stage 4) were weighted up to represent all those included on the frame (stage 2).

Two factors cause a loss of eligible establishments, that is those containing potentially disabled permanent residents, in moving from stage 2 to stage 4: the sampling as such and the failure of selected establishments to respond or co-operate in the inquiry.

The first of these is simply dealt with, by weighting up the selected establishments, but whereas in the private household sample we were able to use an independent estimate of the total population size, for communal establishments no such estimate is

available. The best source of information is therefore the survey itself, so the sampling fraction was used to weight up the selected establishments. Since we have no information whatever about those establishments which did not respond, these are treated in the same way as establishments which were not selected in the sample.

These three steps result in just two weights: 101 for disabled people in small establishments and 304 for those in large establishments.

Note finally that we were unable to weight back to the total population (stage 1) for this sample since, as explained in Chapter 6, certain types of establishment were deliberately excluded from the sampling frame. Chief among these were prisons and military establishments so for these and the other excluded establishments we have no estimate of either the total size or the number of disabled residents. It seemed inappropriate to assume that this rather disparate group of establishments shared the same disability rate as either of our two main samples, so we have excluded them totally from our national estimates of numbers of disabled people.

8.4 Combining estimates from the two samples
The survey aims to produce estimates of national totals for the private household population and, separately, for communal establishments. These two estimates can be added to produce an overall estimate of the total number of disabled adults in Great Britain. As noted earlier in section 6.3, however, not all communal establishments were included in the survey, those which we expected to house very few disabled people and also prisons, which hold few elderly people, were deliberately excluded. Thus our combined estimate, like our estimate for communal establishments, explicitly assumes that there are no disabled people in these excluded establishments.

Another issue arises in relation to prevalence rates. Because the establishments included in the survey are so different from those we excluded, we believe it would be totaly misleading to produce a prevalence rate for all types of communal establishment. On the other hand a prevalence rate for the included establishments, many of which cater exclusively for disabled people, would be equally uninformative. For these reasons, we have not shown prevalence estimates for communal establishments, but we have for both the private household population and for the total population, again explicitly assuming that there are no disabled people in the excluded types of establishment. Our estimate of the total prevalence rate is thus the survey estimate of the total number of disabled adults divided by the total, uncorrected, adult population.

8.5 Investigation of non-response bias
We had no check on non-response bias in the sample of addresses in urban areas which were screened by

personal visits. However, as mentioned earlier, such bias was thought particularly likely to affect the sample screened by post, both because of the method itself and because of the anticipated lower response rate in the postal part of the sample. The follow-up of one in ten of addresses which did not respond to the postal approach allowed us to form an estimate of this source of non-response bias with respect to disability.

To do this we compared disability rates within age-groups for the main postal sift sample and the non-response sample followed up by interviewers. We cannot directly compare the proportions from the first screening phase because in general interviewers identified lower proportions of people as disabled than those identified from the postal questionnaires. The interviewers were able to carry out more checking to determine whether someone ought to be included, whereas at the postal phase all doubtful cases were included as disabled provisionally, so that an interviewer would be able to check at the next phase.

The crucial comparison is therefore between the proportions in different age-groups who were later identified as disabled. Figure 8.3 shows the rates of disability for the main sample screened by post and the sample of non-respondents followed up by interviewers.

For the main postal sample the rates for each age-group rise smoothly with age. As might be expected, the trend with age is not so smooth for the very much smaller non-response sample, although the same general trend is apparent. Chi-square tests show that the difference in the overall distributions were not statistically significant at the 5% level. Moreover, if the non-response follow-up sample is suitably weighted and included in the estimation process the effect on the estimate of the total number of disabled people is negligible. For these reasons the non-response follow-up sample was not used further in the estimation process.

Fig 8.3   Rates of disability by age: main postal sift sample and non-response follow-up sample

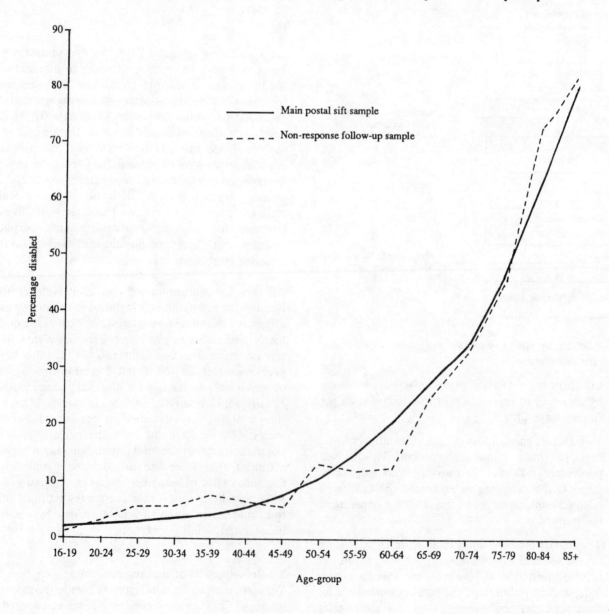

Appendix Sampling errors

A.1 Introduction

Like all estimates based on probability samples, the results of these surveys are subject to random variations termed sampling error. The size of the error depends on a number of factors: the sample size, the sample design, the use made of weighting and the type of survey estimate. A numerical measure of the probable margin of error due to sampling is provided by the quantity known as the standard error, otherwise the square root of the variance.

The sample estimate and its standard error allow us to construct interval estimates with prescribed confidence that the interval includes the average of all possible samples which, in the absence of any bias, will be the true population value. To illustrate this, if all possible samples were selected using the same procedures as here then approximately 19/20 of the intervals from two standard errors below the estimate to two standard errors above it would include the population value.

For any particular sample the confidence interval may or may not include the true value; we can only say that, in the absence of bias, it does contain the true value with 95% confidence.

Two types of survey estimate are presented in this report—population totals (*grossed* estimates) and prevalence rates of disability. The prevalence rates presented here divide the grossed estimates by *known* population figures. It follows that the size of the standard error relative to the estimate is the same for these two types of estimate, so the description below will only treat grossed estimates.

A.2 Private household sample

The basic method of estimating sampling errors from this survey is described in OPCS' Sampling Errors Manual[2]. This method is appropriate to any multi-stage stratified sample, weighted or not, where ratio estimates are employed.

The justification for treating our grossed estimates as ratio estimates is that the weight, described in Chapter 8, takes the form of a known population total divided by a sample total. Thus the grossed estimates, which are simply weighted sample counts of disabled people, take the form of a ratio of two survey counts, multiplied by a constant.

The formula for any of the 15 age-groups used in the weighting procedure can be written

$$\text{Var}(d) = \sum_{s=1}^{17} k_s / 2(k_s - 1) *$$

$$\left[\sum_{i=1}^{k_s - 1} \left\{ (d_{s,i+1} - d_{s,i}) - d/n \, (n_{s,i+1} - n_{s,i}) \right\}^2 \right]$$

where k_s is the number of sectors selected from a particular stratum, s,

$d_{s,i}$ is the grossed number of disabled people in sector i,

$n_{s,i}$ is the weighted number of sift respondents in sector i,

d is the grossed estimate (summed over all sectors), and

n is the weighted number of sift respondents (summed over all sectors).

Two complications arise in the current situation. First, the fact that this is a two-phase sample means that the weights appropriate to the numerator, the count of disabled people, and the denominator, the count in the sift sample are different. For the latter only the third component of the weight, that for inflating the sift sample to the population, was used.

Secondly, the use of separate control totals for the 15 age-groups, although introduced solely for the purpose of reducing a possible non-response bias, incidentally reduces the sampling error of the estimates based on combinations of age-groups. The technique, known in this context as *post-stratification*, had a relatively small effect here, reducing the standard errors of the estimates for all ages combined by between 0% and 6%.

The formula for the variance of a post-stratified grossed estimate is:

$$\text{Var}\left(\sum_p d^{[p]} \right)$$

$$= \sum_p \text{Var}\left(d^{[p]} \right) + \sum_{p \neq q} \sum \text{Cov}\left(d^{[p]}, d^{[q]} \right)$$

where $d^{[p]}$ and $d^{[q]}$ are the grossed estimates from any two post-strata. The covariance terms are estimated in a similar way to the variances of the individual age-groups. The details are given in the reference.

A.3 Communal establishments sample

The simple form of weight employed in this sample means that grossed estimates are no longer ratio estimates and that a simpler method of estimating sampling errors is appropriate. Also the smaller amount of stratification used in this sample leads to a different formula shown below. The complications of the sift and post-stratification referred to above do not arise here.

The formula is:

$$\text{Var}\,(d) = \sum_{s=1}^{17} m_s / (m_s - 1) \sum_{j=1}^{m_s} (d_{s,\,j} - \bar{d}_s)^2$$

where m_s is the number of co-operating establishments in stratum s,

$d_{s,j}$ is the grossed number of disabled people in establishment j,

$\bar{d}_s$ is the mean of the $d_{s,j}$ in the stratum s, and

d is the grossed estimate (summed over all establishments).

A.4 Combining estimates from the two samples

Since the two samples are independent and cover different sections of the population, both the grossed estimates and their variances can be added to produce estimates for the whole population. Prevalence estimates are recalculated from the combined grossed estimates.

Reference

1 Butcher, B and Elliot, D (1987) *A Sampling Errors Manual*. OPCS.

Bibliography on the meaning and measurement of disability with particular reference to health surveys.

American Medical Association (1984) *Guides to the evaluation of permanent impairment*, 2nd ed., Chicago, Ill. A.M.A.

Australian Bureau of Statistics (1981) *Survey of Handicapped Persons, Australia, February—May, 1981 (Preliminary)*, 17 August, Canberra.

Badley, E M, Thompson, R P and Wood, P H N (1978). The Prevalence and Severity of Major Disabling Conditions—A Reappraisal of the Government Social Survey on the Handicapped and Impaired in Great Britain, *International Journal of Epidemiology*, 7, No. 2, 145–151.

Bebbington, A C (1977) Scaling indices of disablement. *Journal of Preventative and Social Medicine*, 31, No. 2, 122–126.

Benjamin, J (1976) The Northwick Park A D L Index, *Occupational Therapy*, Dec, 301–6.

Blaxter, M (1976) *The Meaning of Disability*, London: Heinemann.

Bonte, J T P (1973) *The Use of ICIDH Classifications in Health Interview Surveys*, WHO.

Bruett, T L and Overs, R P (1969) A Critical Review of 12 ADL Scales. *Physical Therapy*, 49, 857–862.

Cartwright, A (1983) *Health Surveys in practice and potential.* London: Kings Fund Publishing Office.

Charlton, J R H, Patrick D L and Peach, H. Use of multivariate measures of disability in health surveys, *Journal of Epidemiology and Community Health*, 1983, 37, 296–304.

Chrichton Royal Behavioural Rating Scale (Modified) (n.d.) Wittington Hospital, Manchester.

Cullinan, T R (1976) *The Epidemiology of Visual Impairment, Part II. Visually Handicapped in Canterbury 1974*, Health Services Research Unit, University of Kent.

Cullinan, T (1986) *Visual Disability in the Elderly*, London: Croom Helm.

Department of Health (1981) *Physical Disability: Results of a Survey in the Wellington Hospital Board Area*, Special Report Series, 59, Wellington.

Department of Health and Social Security (1970) *Handbook for Industrial Injuries Medical Boards.* London: HMSO.

Department of Health and Social Security (1976) *Handbook for War Pensions Medical Boards*: London: DHSS

Department of Health and Social Security (1976) *Classification and Assessment of Impairment and Handicap. Note of a meeting.* Unpublished Report, London: DHSS.

Dinnerstein, A J, Lowenthal, M and Dexter, M (1965) Evaluation of a Rating Scale of Ability in Activities of Daily Living, *Archives of Physical Medicine and Rehabilitation*, 46, 579–84.

Donaldson, S W (1973) A Unified ADL Evaluation Form. *Archives of Physical and Medical Rehabilitation*, 54, 175–179.

Duckworth, D (1983) *Some problems in using the ICIDH to obtain statistical data*, WHO.

Duckworth, D (1983) *DHSS Social Research Branch, Research Report No. 10, The Classification and Measurement of Disablement*, London: HMSO.

Duckworth, D Knight, R and Warren M D (1984) Using the ICIDH in household surveys; problems and possibilities, *Statistical Journal of the United Nations*, ECE, 2, 85–96.

Ebrahim, S, Nouri, F and Barer, D (1985) Measuring disability after a stroke. *Journal of Epidemiology and Community Health*, 39, 86–89.

Gallin, R S and Given, C W. The Concept and Classification of Disability in Health Interview Surveys, *Inquiry*, 13, No 4, 395–407.

Garrad, J and Bennett, A E (1971). A validated interview schedule for use in population surveys of chronic disease and disability. *British Journal of Preventative and Social Medicine*, 25, 97–104.

Government of India, National Sample Survey Organisation, (1983), *Report on survey of disabled persons*, Department of Statistics, New Delhi.

Graham, P A and Wallace, J (1968) Evaluation of postal detection of registrable blindness. *British Journal of Preventative and Social Medicine*, 238–241.

Greenwood, J G (1985) Disability dilemmas and rehabilitation tensions: a twentieth century inheritance, *Social Science and Medicine*, 20, No. 12, 1241–1252.

Haber, L D (1967) Identifying The Disabled: Concepts and Methods in the Measurement of Disability, *Social Security Bulletin*, 30, No. 12, 17–34.

Haggard, M, Gatehouse, S and Davis, A (1981). The High Prevalence of Hearing Disorders and its Implications for Services in the UK, *British Journal of Audiology*, 15, 241–251.

Hansluwka, H E (1985) Measuring the health of populations, indicators and interpretations. *Social Science and Medicine*, 20, No. 12, 1207–1224.

Harris, A I (1971) *Handicapped and Impaired in Great Britain*, London: HMSO.

Hunter, J (1986) What does 'virtually unable to walk' mean? *British Medical Journal*, 292, 172–173.

Hutchinson, T P (1985) Analysing severity data when assessors differ in their usage of the categories. *The Statistician*, 34, 183–195.

Jagger, C, Clarke, M and Davies, R A (1986). The elderly at home: indices of disability, *Journal of Epidemiology and Community Health*, 40, 139–142.

Jefferys, M *et al* (1969). A set of tests for measuring motor impairment in prevalence studies. *Journal of Chronic Diseases*, 22, 303–319.

Katin, R L, Goldfarb, A I, Pollock, M and Peck, A (1960) Brief objective measures for the determination of mental status of the aged. American *Journal of Psychiatry*, 117, 326.

Katz, S *et al* (1963) Studies of Illness in the Aged; The Index of ADL: A standardized measure of Biological and Psychosocial Function. *Journal of the American Medical Association*, 185, No. 12, 914–919.

Kind, P, Rosser, R and Williams, A, (1982) Valuation of quality of life: some psychometric evidence. In *Value of Life and Safety*, Jones-Lee, MW (ed) Geneva Association.

Kirscht, J P (1971) Social and Psychological problems of surveys of health and illness, *Social Science and Medicine*, 5, 519–526.

Kleijn-de Vrankrijker, M de (1983) *Using the ICIDH in Interview Surveys*, WHO.

Knight, R and Warren, M D (1978) *DHSS Report on Health and Social Subjects, Physically Disabled People Living at Home: A Study of Numbers and Needs*. London: HMSO.

Krischer, J P (1979) Indexes of Severity: Conceptual Development, *Health Services Research*, 56–66.

Lees, D and Shaw, S (1974) (eds) *Impairment, Disability and Handicap*, London: HEB.

Locker, D, Wiggins, R, Sittamplan, Y and Patrick, D L (1981) Estimating the prevalence of disability in the community: the influence of sample design and response bias, *Journal of Epidemiology and Community Health*, 35, 208–212.

Mahoney, F I and Barthel, D W (1965) Functional Evaluation: The Barthel Index, Rehabilitation Notes, *Maryland State Medical Journal*, Feb, 61–64.

Nicholls II, W L (1979) *California Disability Survey: Technical Report*, Survey Research Centre, University of California, Berkeley.

Patrick, D L (1981) *Health and care of the physically disabled in Lambeth. The longitudinal disability interview survey. Phase I Report*. London: Department of Community Medicine, St Thomas' Hospital Medical School.

Patrick, D L (1982) *Health and care of the physically disabled in Lambeth. The longitudinal disability interview survey. Phase II Report*. London: Department of Community Medicine, St Thomas' Medical School.

Patrick, D L *et al* (1981) Screening for disability in the inner city, *Journal of Epidemiology and Community Health*, 35, 65–70.

Patrick, D L *et al* (1985) A Cross-cultural comparison of Health Status Values. *American Journal of Public Health*, 75, No. 12, 1402–1407.

Patrick, D L, Somerville, S and Sittamplan, Y (n.d.) *Assessing the severity of dysfunctional behaviours: A value scaling study of the Functional Limitations Profile*, Unpublished.

Peach, H *et al* (1980) Evaluation of a postal screening questionnaire to identify the physically disabled, *International Rehabilitation Medicine*, 2, 189–193.

Pope, C R (1984) Disability and health status: the importance of longitudinal studies, *Social Science and Medicine*, 19, No. 6, 589–593.

Rosnow, I and Breslau, N (1966) A Gultman Health Scale for the Aged. *Journal of Gerontology*, 21, No. 4 556–9.

Rosser, R and Kind, P (1978). A Scale of Valuations of States of Illness: is there a Social Consensus? *International Journal of Epidemiology*, 7 No. 4, 347–358.

Sainsbury, S (1973) *Measuring Disability, Occasional Papers on Social Administration*, London: G. Bell and Sons.

Schroedel, J G (1984) Analysing surveys on deaf adults: implications of survey research on persons with disabilities. *Social Science and Medicine*, 19, No. 6, 619–627.

Selman, M and Barnitt, R (1983) Measuring Disability by means of ADL Indices. *Occupational Therapy*, August, 225–227.

Snaith, R P and Hamilton, M (1976) *British Journal of Psychiatry*, 128, 156–165.

Sokolow, M D *et al* (1985) Functional Approach to Disability Evaluation. *The Journal of the American Medical Association*, 167, No. 13, 1575–1584.

Somerville, S M, Silver, R and Patrick, D L (1983) Services for disabled people. What criteria should we use to assess disability! *Community Medicine*, 5, 302–310.

Stein, R E K (1987) Severity of illness: concepts and measurements, *The Lancet*, December 26.

Stewart, A L *et al* (1981) Advances in the Measurement of Functional Status: Construction of Aggregate Indexes. *Medical Care*, XIX, No. 5, 473–488.

Terry, M A and Jones, D M (1983) Estimation of Loudness by Questionnaire, *Journal of Applied Psychology*, 68, No. 2, 273–277.

Torrance, G W (1976) Social Preferences for health states: an empirical evaluation of three measurement techniques *Socio-economic Planning Science*, 10, 129–136.

Van den Berg, J and Van Sonsbeck, J L A (1983), *Experiences with the OECD long-term disability indicator: use in fieldwork and coding in IDH categories*, WHO.

Warren, M D (1974). *The Canterbury Survey of Handicapped People, Report No 6*, Health Services Research Unit, University of Kent, Canterbury.

Warren, M D (1976). Interview surveys of handicapped people: the accuracy of statements about the underlying medical conditions. *Rheumatology and Rehabilitation*, 15, 295–302.

Warren, M D (1985). The Canterbury studies of disablement in the community; prevalence needs and attitudes. *International Journal of Rehabilitation Research*, 8, 3–18.

Warren, M D (1987). The Prevalence of Disability: Measuring and Estimating the Number and the Needs of Disabled People in the Community, *Public Health*, 101, 333–341.

Warren, M D, Knight, R and Warren, J L (1979) *Changing Capabilities and Needs of People with Handicaps. A two-year Follow-up Study. Report No. 39*, Health Services Research Unit, University of Kent, Canterbury.

Whitehead, A (1981) Identification of the Disabled Person. In Disability: *Legislation and Practice*, (ed) D Guthrie (1981) London: MacMillan.

Williams, R G A (1979) Theories and measurement in disability, *Epidemiology and Community Health*, 33, 32–47.

Williams, R G A (1983) Disability as health indicator. In *Health Indicators*, (ed) A J Culyer (1983), Oxford.

Wood, P N H and Badley, E M (1978). An epidemiological appraisal of disablement. *In Recent Advances in Community Medicine I*, (ed) Bennett, A E, London: Churchill Livingstone

Wood, P H N and Badley, E M (1980) People with disabilities—*Towards acquiring information which reflects more sensitively their problems and needs*. World Rehabilitation Fund.

World Health Organisation (1980), *International classification of Impairments, Disabilities and Handicaps*, Geneva: WHO.

Wylie, C M and White, B K (1964). A measure of disability. *Archives of Environmental Health*, 8, 834–839.

RECENT REPORTS FROM OPCS
Social Survey Division

Smoking among secondary school children in 1986

by Eileen Goddard and Clare Ikin

This third national survey of smoking among secondary school children looks at smoking prevalence and behaviour and explores their attitudes towards smoking.

ISBN 0 11 691208 1   Price £8.20 net

Improving electoral registration
and
Electoral registration in inner city areas, 1983-1984

by Jean Todd and Jack Eldridge

Two reports on the subject of electoral registration, one of field trials of a re-designed Form A and the other investigating the accuracy of the electoral register in areas which were thought to present particular problems to the compilers.

ISBN 0 11 691204 9   Price £4.60 net
ISBN 0 11 691203 0   Price £5.40 net

Informal carers

by Hazel Green

Carried out as a part of the General Household Survey 1985, this report estimates the numbers and characteristics of people who are providing informal care to a sick, handicapped or elderly person living in their own or another household.

ISBN 0 11 691226 X   Price £3.75 net

HMSO BOOKS

Available from HMSO Bookshops and Agents (see Yellow Pages) or through any good bookshop. In case of difficulty, write to:
HMSO Books (P9D) St Crispins, Duke Street, Norwich NR3 1PD

Printed in the United Kingdom for Her Majesty's Stationery Office
Dd290093 10/89 C8 G443 10170